FOUR TIMES NEW YORK TIMES BUSINESS BEST SELLING AUTHOR:
WALL STREET MONEY MACHINE, BUSINESS BUY THE BIBLE and
REAL ESTATE MONEY MACHINE, 101 WAYS TO BUY REAL ESTATE WITHOUT CASH

HOW TO PICK UP
FORECLOSURES

"My Step-By-Step Guide
to Get Super Discounted
Real Estate Before
the Auction"

WADE B. COOK

"This publication is designed to provide accurate and authoritative
information in regard to the subject matter covered. It is sold with the
understanding that the publisher is not engaged in advice or other
expert assistance is required, the service. If legal advice or other
expert assistance is required, the services of a competent professional
person should be sought."

From a declaration of principles jointly adopted by a committee of the
American Bar Association and committee of the Publisher' Association

Library of Congress Cataloging in Publication data
Cook, Wade
How to Pick Up Foreclosures
1. Real Estate INvestment. I. Title.
HD......

Liberty Network, Incorporated
1420 NW Gilman Blvd., Suite 2131
Issaquah, WA 98027

Distributed by
Midpoint Trade Books, Inc.
212-727-0190

ISBN 0-9745749-1-0

Printed in the United States of America
Third Edition
10 9 8 7 6 5 4 3 2 1

Other Books
by Wade B. Cook

Real Estate Money Machine
Real Estate for Real People
101 Ways to Buy Real Estate Without Cash
Cook's Book on Creative Real Estate

Wall Street Money Machine
Stock Market Miracles
Free Stocks: How to get the Stock Market to Pay for your Stocks
Safety First Investing
Wade Cook's Stock Picking Handbook
Red Light, Green Light
A+
Business Buy the Bible
Success: American Style
Brilliant Deductions
Wealth 101
Don't Set Goals (the old way)
Wade Cook's Power Quotes
Mangosteen: Shocking Discoveries

Coming Soon
Get in Touch With Your Inner Millionaire
Stock Market Money Machine

*To Laura, the one who still
makes my heart skip a beat every time I see her.*

Acknowledgements

This book has been a long time in process. So many people have helped me, both during the investing and in the writing process. I would like to thank them. First, my wife Laura, who has edited and typed and given me much encouragement. Next, the rest of the office staff who pushed me to do more, and who do so much to lighten my load.

Contents

Preface

THE HAND DOESN'T COME VERY FAR OUT
OF THE GRAVE TO CONTROL ANYTHING.

Preface

When I first started investing, I kept hearing about other people's formulas and how they were going to get rich by doing one thing or another, or make all kinds of money on that kind of property. I went to lectures and heard people present formulas to use in evaluating property, in determining whether a certain investment was going to be a good deal by looking at it from different angles.

I quickly realized that the only thing I could understand, because of my inexperience, was actual value. I was going to have to find the properties that had built-in equity, in terms of easy fix-up properties that, with a little cosmetic work, could increase a lot in value.

In the beginning I didn't go out looking for foreclosure properties because I didn't know they even existed. After talking with different homeowners, and realizing the problems that many of them were getting into because of their house payments, I realized this might be a profitable investment avenue. Because of various problems, people wanted to unload properties, and unload them with excellent terms.

I started to realize that if I was going to make big money on any one property, it was going to be in some kind of distress sale. There are three main types of distress sales. First, the owner needs to relocate immediately. This is usually due to a job change. The second type of distressed property is a house that is in need of repairs, and the owner has run out of energy, time, or even the money to do the repairs. The third type of distressed property is when people come up against some kind of financial difficulty in their lives and are on the verge of losing the property because payments haven't been made. I started looking into this scenario by asking questions of people who were familiar with this area of real estate. I realized there was an active foreclosure market.

I started to call on people who were about to lose their property at some kind of foreclosure sale. I found them by simply reading an advertisement in my local paper. In most cases, even though the property was listed in the legal notices, there was nobody living on the property. As I tracked down people to find out all I could about these properties, the system became easy. I was able to pick up many of these properties at great prices.

The sheer leverage of getting into these properties by picking up just the back payments and a few of the court costs to that date, made them extremely good deals. It also helped the people who were losing their houses; they would not be foreclosed on and it would save their credit rating. It would also stop the banks from bugging them. They might have lived in the house for up to a year without paying any monthly payments, and now they were able to walk away and not have to worry about how it was going to affect them in the future, because I stopped the foreclosure.

After dealing with these types of properties for several years, I am under the impression that the best time to pick them up is before they are on the auction block; before anything drastic takes place and they are given back to or taken back by the bank. Later in this book I will cover some of the procedures for picking these properties up at the auction or at the trustee's sale or sheriffs sale. I developed a step by step process for not only locating these properties, but finding information about the properties and the homeowners. This information became very valuable to some of my friends and clients who were investing in real estate at the time. And now, as I have traveled around the country extensively as a lecturer and have been asked repeatedly about foreclosures, I have felt that it is time that a book of this nature be written to show people not only the beauty of these types of properties, but of the MO for finding them.

This book will not generalize on real estate, and yet there will be several interesting concepts of real estate taught throughout the book. Some of the concepts will be valuable in any pursuit.

I have said time and time again, if a person wants to become an expert, real estate is probably the best area in which to gain expertise. Not only is it fun and exciting, but real estate also has a very high rate of return. If you choose real estate, become an expert in finding good value. In all of my years of investing, I have found the largest values can be found in foreclosures.

Chapter 1

The Time Line

Chapter 1

The Time Line

Before we get into the step by step process of how to find and process foreclosed properties, it would be well to understand what has happened to such a property. Let us see what will happen to this property in the future, and find out where on that timeline we can step into the picture.

Let us go to the beginning and see some of the problems that people incur. We will not only talk about these to show the beginning of the foreclosure time line, but also to lead the investor to the people who are having problems with their properties.

Obviously, a person does not buy a house thinking that he is going to be foreclosed on. At the time that he buys the house, all the information that he has given to the bank, FHA or VA has been truthful. But if there is one thing that is constant in this life, it is that nothing is constant, everything changes. Unexpected things pop up in peoples' lives that they are not prepared for, causing undue difficulties. A person might lose a job, get sick, or have a death in the family. Because of these things, the payments stop. Then the person is quickly forced into a foreclosure sale.

Whatever the cause, the person quits making payments on the house. However, I have never seen anybody quit making payments on a house, with a thought of losing it. They felt that it was a temporary situation. They all felt that something would happen, something would change and they would be able to pull some kind of magic money out of their sleeve, curing the loan, and solving the problems with their house.

Many people think of house payments as if they were rent payments and they pay their house payments as if they were merely tenants. This is especially true with new homeowners. When money gets tight, the first area many people cut back on is the house payment.

The bank or lender obviously becomes very upset. They start writing nice letters at the beginning of the problem; trying to be kind so that the people will keep their savings account deposits with their bank. Then, after a month or two or three, the bank sends a notice that they are going to turn this over to their legal office to handle the problem. In this letter will be a strict warning of the things which can happen. The worst case is that the house will be taken away.

If the homeowner tries to make a payment during this time, the bank might accept that payment and then proceed, suing the people anyway. Most likely they will send the payment back and demand full payment, realizing that if they receive anything they have jeopardized their position. (What they would be saying is that it is not okay for the homeowner to make late payments.) All payments, including the cost now of filing and sending such letters, will have to be paid in order for the loan to be actively reinstated.

If not paid, an attorney or representative of the lending institution has the papers turned over to him. He will immediately send out letters stating that he has been hired by the bank or the lending institution to act in the bank's behalf. He will usually give several alternatives to the homeowner in this letter, i.e., if you will pay the back payments by a specific date, it will be such and such an amount, but if you wait and pay the back payments by a later date, (which may be a couple months later and right before the foreclosure sale) then the payments and the costs will be so much more.

The person who is representing the bank will be required by law to file some kind of legal public notice. This may be done in the legal journal for the whole country, or may be done in the local newspaper at the beginning or end of the classified section. In most states, this ad will have to run up to five or six times and usually once a week for a specified time before the actual trustee's sale or sheriff's sale.

This notification or announcement will state all the parties involved, the type of loan, mortgage, deed of trust or whatever legal document that is being foreclosed on. It will state the date that the sale will take place. It will usually include the latest date by which the problem can be taken care of, which is usually called the cure date.

It will also include the common address and legal description of the property. If it does not include the address, it is a simple matter of going to a title company or the county courthouse and looking up the legal description and finding the common address. It will also include the name of the attorney or the representative handling the sale and his/her phone number.

Now that these ads are placed, time goes on, and the person is still not making the payments. In most cases, the person now understands that he is in trouble and will probably lose the house. He will usually move out of the house rather than be hassled by the banks and people knocking on his door trying to get him to make up the monthly payments.

Many of today's loans are not good ones to assume, because you will be assuming the same problems (huge monthly payments) that the original owners are having. But, with these types of loans, the banks are starting to realize that they do not want to take these properties back. They might seem gruff, but getting these properties back only creates new problems and their people sometimes work with these homeowners in anyway that they can. If a property passes the cure date, it now goes to a trustee sale. It has passed the cure date. In most states the only person who would be able to cure after the cure date is the actual homeowner. Now the trustee or the attorney for the trustee, the beneficiary of the deed of trust or the mortgage, or even the Sheriff will go to the county courthouse, the city building, or wherever the legal records are kept for the county, and will stand in view of the public and auction it off. They will say, "I, as attorney for _____, representing _____, am here to auction off to the highest bidder, the property located at:_____." He will then proceed to read the legal description of the property.

He will also state the amount of the loan, the mortgage balance, the interest that is due and owing, and the amount of the court costs and foreclosure costs up to that time. He will lump them together in one sum and then state the total that the trustee bids. He will ask for any other bids, and if there is nobody there, he will say, "Going once, going twice, trustee takes possession, gone." At that point in time, he will notify the Sheriff of these proceedings. The Sheriff will order a writ of possession and now the homeowner has lost his house.

If the homeowner does not leave the house, the Sheriffs department will go there with the truck that has the big star on the side and proceed to evict the people from the house. They will then impound everything in the house, including the furniture, the food, and the garbage. It will cost the homeowner several hundred dollars to get his things out of impoundment. If the person goes back on the property, he risks being arrested and put in jail.

He can have nothing now to do with the property. The bank is now in possession of the property.

The reason I have gone through this step by step, is to show the gruesome side of the process. I want to find these properties long before they get to the sale. I have stood on the sidewalk watching a young family with their three children lose their house. They thought they could save the house. They could not. They just kept ignoring the announcements and then, there they were, standing on the sidewalk in tears, the little kids were allowed to keep their big wheels because the Sheriffs deputies were nice. I stood there on the sidewalk and cried with this family. It was really sad. I realized then that if I could be more persuasive in talking to people, I could get them to understand that I was willing to give them a little bit of money, at least enough to get them set up in another place, and save their credit rating.

Now, on the time line, where do you fit in? If you could find out about this property before the announcements are sent out--in the beginning when the people are just starting to get the late payment notices, and if they realized they could not make up the back payments, they might be willing to sell or just deed it to you, rather than lose the house. If they knew that they were not going to be able to cure it, then this is one point where you could come into the picture.

Another entry point would be after the house is already in some state of foreclosure, but before the cure date. The only way to do it then is to deal with the attorney or the representative of the bank who is handling the sale. You may come into the time line after the cure date only by attending the auction. There are obviously better places than others to come into the picture. In the later chapters, we will see how to get there first and how to process things before they ever get to the state of being auctioned off.

Publisher's Note

Available now is the complete *Pre-Foreclosure System* on four hours of a CD home study course. It also contains all the forms, documents and explanations that will help you establish your own step-by-step system of getting foreclosure properties before the auction. This is the most definitive foreclosure system available today. You can order this system by calling:

Liberty Network, Inc.
1420 N.W. Gilman Blvd.#2131
Issaquah, Washington 98027
425-222-3760

Ask for the *Pre-Foreclosures System CD set*. Visa, and Mastercard holders may call 1-866-579-5900 and ask for the Pre-Foreclosures System CD home study course.

THE ACTUAL TIME LINE

AUCTION
cure date

calm before
the storm

legal notices start

letters form attorney

letters from bank

PROBLEM
STARTS

Months	1	2	3	4	5	6	7	8	9
Monthly Payment	$700	$700	$700	$700	$700	$700	$700	$700	NO
Late Payment	30	30	30	30	30	30	30	30	NO
Foreclosure Costs			50	25	100	100	50	50	NO
Total to Cure	$730	$1,460	$2,240	$2,995	$3,825	$4,655	$5,425	$6,215	$6,215

This example depicts the urgency of stopping the foreclosure proceedings in its early stages. The earlier stopped, the better the leverage.

"Martha get the piggy bank, the sheriff just pulled up."

AUCTION

"If only someone would lend me the money to save it."

"Where is that guy who wanted this place?"

"I don't care whose attorney you are, Joe at the bank is my friend."

"Please, Joe, accept this one back payment."

"Mom, can you loan me some money?"

"I hate these letters from the bank."

"I'd better get a new job."

"I've been a few payments behind before."

9

8

7

6

5

4

3

2

1

Months

THE TIME LINE FOR THE HOMEOWNER

PROBLEM STARTS

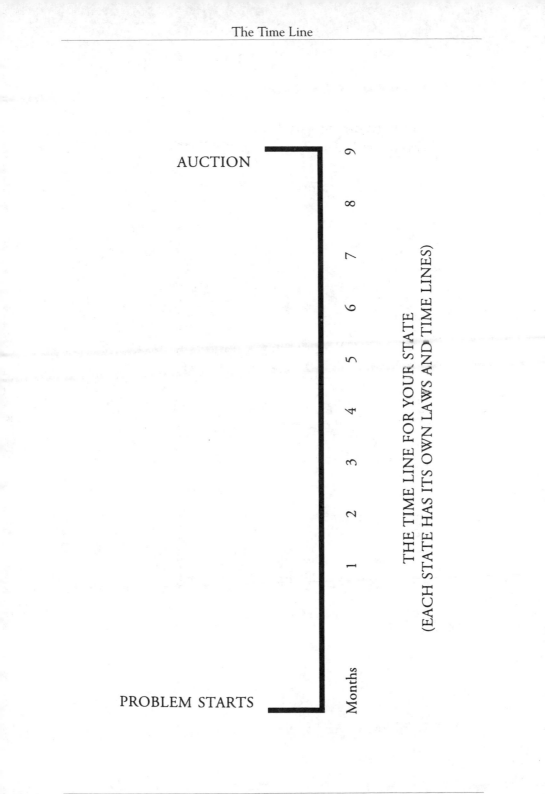

AUCTION

PROBLEM STARTS

Months

1 2 3 4 5 6 7 8 9

THE TIME LINE FOR YOUR STATE
(EACH STATE HAS ITS OWN LAWS AND TIME LINES)

"OH, BUT MY MOTHER-IN-LAW IN NEW
JERSEY WILL SEND THE MONEY."

Chapter 2

The Personal Side
of the Homeowner

YOU DIDN'T CREATE THE SITUATION, BUT YOU _CAN_ THROW OUT A SAFETY NET.

Chapter 2

The Personal Side of the Homeowner

In order to understand what kind of solutions we are going to bring to the homeowner's life, you need to look at the problem from his point of view. You need to see what is going on, and then see not only what has happened, but what is going to happen.

He has lived on this property and has not been making his monthly payments on it. He has been harassed by the bank quite a bit to make up these payments. Most people are resilient in the face of bad times, so much so that they think that they can solve their problems, and most people do solve their problems. The house now starts into the foreclosure process, but very few of those are actually foreclosed on.

I was talking to an attorney one time and he said that he processed 20 to 30 foreclosures a week. Once they get into the third and fourth month of the time line, they are usually cured by the owner. He has even had weeks go by where all of them were cured before the cure date. Now, however, more and more people are not able to cure their loans.

They used to be able to get easy money from many banks or from their credit unions. Since those sources of loans have dried up, these people are not able to solve their problems. Most then turn to relatives to come up with the money. If those relatives do not have the money, they might attempt to borrow the money. If the source of money from the relatives also dry up, this causes a bad situation for the homeowner. If he gets behind the eight ball, it is very hard to get out in front again.

Let us look at some of the things that will happen to the homeowner if the foreclosure goes through and he actually loses his house. The big one is his credit rating. In most states, a person with a minor problem of late monthly payments (for instance, late payment on a Mastercard or Visa) will have that stay on his credit report for three years. A major foreclosure like this will stay on his credit report for up to seven years.

What that means is that he will have to do a lot of explaining to buy another house. He also runs the risk of not being able to buy another house for seven years, especially if money stays as tight as it is right now and banks continue to be very choosy about selecting people to give loans to.

I met with a guy named Joe one time. He was going to lose his house. It was already in the far stages of foreclosure. As I was talking to him, he kept saying something was going to happen; his mother-in-law in New Jersey was going to send him money or he was going to be able to get a loan. He had applications in for five or six loans around town at different banks.

It got down to about two days before the cure date and all of his sources of funds were falling through. I said, "Look, you are having a bad time right now. You have lost your job, you are out of work, but you are not going to be that way for very long and you already have a good possibility of a new job in Oregon. Why don't you cut your losses now and move on? Do not make things worse.

Suck it in. Why mess up your life for the next seven years and not be able to buy another house because of the problems you are having right now?"

The mentality of these people is: "This cannot be happening to me." They do not realize that these banks are playing their own game of making money. That is how they justify themselves; that is how they stay in business. The typical bank will have thousands of loans, and here is one person who is causing a problem.

A bank has a staff of people who probably spend more time worrying about these few houses than they do on all of the good loans and all of the good payments they have coming in. The banks are not in a position to play games and keep waiting for people. They expect that once people have made promises, the promises will be kept.

These homeowners do not understand that. Most people are very forgiving. They see another person having problems and they forgive him. They say, "Oh, sure, that's okay, make up the payments whenever you can. We will work through this problem together." Banks are not in that position. People that are being foreclosed on think that they are dealing with another person and they do not realize that these banks can be very ruthless.

People think that they can walk in and tell the bank that they have a new job and things are going to be fine, but unless they are talking cash, the banks are not willing to listen. This is especially true now when banks are so concerned about cash and banks previously have gone out of business because of their cash flow situations. They are not willing to negotiate with people and work out any kind of deal at all. Banks function on one premise: that they can foreclose on the property and get back in control. When I was out showing some people the actual foreclosure notification, they could not believe it was happening. One time I sat with a man and showed him the announcement. The whole ad was 10 inches long because of the legal description and the complexity of the documents. I sat there and circled it with a red felt tip pen. I drew several arrows to it and said, "Look right here, your house is going to be sold on this day; here are all the back payments that are due; and here are all the legal processes you would have to go through to save your house." I sat with him for almost two hours and could not convince him that he was going to lose his house.

Peripheral Problems

These misunderstandings, and the problems that come up if the physical structure of the house has not been properly maintained, bring up a personal side to investing that is different from any other type of real estate investing. With most types of property, people are dealing from a position of strength. The buyer and seller have something that each wants; one has a property, one has money, and they are both negotiating for the best possible deal. But when it comes to foreclosures, these people are not dealing from a position of strength; they have much to lose. I do not have a heart of stone, and when I first started investing, it was difficult to go out and talk with these people.

After several attempts, I got to the point where I would not even go after a house after the initial contact with the people if there was any resistance at all. It just wasted too much of my time. There was no way they were going to realize they were losing the property until the Sheriff actually came out and evicted them. I developed a philosophy that the only kind of properties I would go after would be vacant properties. They were very numerous; as a matter of fact, there were more houses going through foreclosure that the people had already moved out of, than there were ones that had people still living in them.

However, at some point in time, if we are going to pick up a house before the cure date and get it for just the back payments and the costs to that date, we are going to have to deal with the people who own the house. The people who stand in the chain of title are the only ones who have the right to convey and deed the property. We are going to have to find them--whether they are in the house or are living in another state. In short, if we want the property, those people are going to have to sign the deed.

In closing this chapter, the investor needs to realize the human side of this problem. You will be dealing with people who are going through a bad part of their lives. You will need to approach them with a great deal of finesse.

Chapter 3

Get There First

WAYS TO GET ATTORNEYS TO GIVE YOU
INFORMATION ON POSSIBLE FORECLOSURES
LONG BEFORE THEY GET SERIOUS.

Chapter 3

Get There First

The way to excel in picking up foreclosures is to track down the property and be in pursuit of having the property deeded to you long before other people get involved in looking at the property. Before I give you the details on how to do this, remember that once many people are bidding on a piece of property the terms will change. You will find yourself doing things that you would not have done had you acquired to the property in the early stages of the time line.

BEFORE THE ANNOUNCEMENT

Long before the legal announcement is ever placed, the present homeowners know that they will be losing their property. Even before they know that they will be actually losing their property, they feel that they are running that risk, and it is at this time that they are willing to talk about a possible sale.

It is also at this time that they are not willing to let you just take over the property for the balance of the loan to save their credit rating. They will want something for the property. The further it moves along the time line the fewer demands they will have. If you can find this property in the early stages, before other people (investors) get into the picture, and offer a reasonable price, you will be in a position to make friends with the people and work out a deal that is satisfactory to both of you.

KEEP YOUR EAR TO THE GROUND

I have picked up properties in several different stages of foreclosure. Few were found through the legal notices. I found these properties simply by being aware that they existed and creating opportunities where I could find them.

The opportunity was created because of the huge volume of business that I was doing. I was constantly talking with people about houses all over town. At times, I was looking at ten to fifteen. houses a day, and would invariably hear about houses that were being foreclosed on or about the people that were going to lose their houses. It was these houses that I gave special attention to and tracked down with extra effort.

It is hard to write in this book where you will find this information. It would be easy to say this information is available on the street, but it's hard to see this if you haven't been there, so let me give you a few specific examples.

REAL ESTATE AGENTS

Often when people realize that they are going to lose their house, they will call real estate agents to see if there is any way of selling it. They will unload on the real estate agent all the information about their plight. They are in dire need to sell the property and in a hurry.

Some agents will be able to help them, but many agents will not be able to help in such a short period of time. These people have let the time elapse to the point of only having a few days left. In talking with real estate agents, you might ask them if they know of anyone who is losing his house or is having a foreclosure processed against them.

This will often plant the seeds that will open up many doors. It will blossom into many transactions that you may be able to process; ones that you normally wouldn't have been able to find. Remember, agent walk a fine line in trying to find good deals for you; they also represent the sellers and are trying to get good deals for them.

ATTORNEYS

As we mentioned before, there are many attorneys who process these trustee sales. It would be good to go to them and find out all of the ones that they are handling. If worked properly, you will be able to get to these houses before they get too far along the time line.

One other point by getting houses in the early stages of the time line you are saving on the payments that have elapsed. The attorneys will get you there first and hopefully they will get you to the right people. They will also be able to inform you of any clause or restrictions on the underlying loans. They should have all the documents for the property, including the original loan papers and the deeds in their file. You will be able to save time and not have to go to a title company or the courthouse to get this information.

FLYERS

In *The Real Estate Money Machine*, I talk about passing out flyers around different neighborhoods. One suggestion mentioned in the flyer "Why You Are Selling Your House", was that people might be selling because of financial difficulties. I was trying to plant the seeds on the flyer and let people know that if they were having financial difficulties they could call me. When I passed out the flyers (and I did so consistently), I repeatedly received phone calls from people who were losing their houses and were in some stage of the foreclosure process. I probably found more houses through this means than any other thing that I tried.

Usually these houses were in the very early stages of foreclosure. Once they had hit foreclosure, or hit the legal notices, I already knew about them from other sources. Flyers work extremely well, and long before anybody else even knew that the people were having problems with the property, I was on their doorstep to see if I could solve their problem.

REMODELERS

There are many people who fix up properties or do remodeling work for others. It is amazing how much information they have about different houses. In the normal course of their business they come across people who are either (a) trying to fix up their house to sell it, or (b) are thinking about doing something with their home; but, they may not be willing to spend the money to fix up the house and will sell it as is.

I had a friend who was in the remodeling business and generated ninety-five percent of his business by getting on the phone every morning to call different people to see if they would like to have any work done on their house. His purpose was to come out and give them an estimate to see if they would use him when they wanted work done.

Many times he would come across people who would say, "No, I was going to fix it up, but I am losing my house to the bank." He would say, "Listen, before you do that, I have a friend who picks up houses and will take it off your hands. He will take it the way it is and stop the problems with the bank. Would you like to talk to him?" If they said yes, then he would give me their name and I would go see them and negotiate a deal. Two or three of the best properties that I ever processed were found in this manner.

SUMMARY

Do whatever it takes to get there first (be as imaginative as you can be). It will save you time and money. This would be a good area to concentrate your efforts on-finding ways to be the first one to the property.

Publisher's Note:

We would like to make a special offer to those of you who have purchased this book.

Many of you will not be able to attend the seminar that Mr. Cook teaches around the country. This is one of the best and most exciting seminars taught and we would like to give you a sampling of what it is like to be there. We have a cd which is about one hour long that will cover, in lecture format, all the concepts of buying, holding, and selling properties, from start-up to the three entity approach, to your retirement. It is Mr. Cook's whole system of investing in real estate. For yours write:

Liberty Network, Inc.
1420 NW Gilman Blvd, Ste# 2130
Washington 98027
1-866-579-5900, 1-425-222-3760

Chapter 4

An Investor's Dream

Chapter 4

An Investor's Dream

Before we move on and get into the thick of things, it would be good to review why picking up foreclosures is good for you as an investor. It would be easy to say that price is the only good reason, but there are a few more.

AREA OF EXPERTISE

Each endeavor undertaken has a system that needs to be adhered to if one wants to be successful. Foreclosures are no different. Processing them is a specialty system, of which bits and pieces may be used elsewhere but, generally speaking, it is a self-contained system.

The vocabulary for processing foreclosures is also unique to this area of investing. Words like "cure date," "auction block," "trustee's sale," "sheriff's sale" and a host of others are used on the street. We've freely used these words throughout the book. If necessary, an explanation accompanies the word, but usually the word can be understood when used in context.

There are also time periods and dates that are only common to foreclosures and auctions. You'll learn quickly how important these dates are. I used to drive around singing, "Just get me to the courthouse on time," as a constant reminder to myself to hustle and not let any dates slip by.

What does all of this mean the modus operandi, the vocabulary, and the dates to you as an investor? First of all, it means that your job of becoming an expert has some clearly defined boundaries.

Never mind real estate as a whole. You can zero in on a part of real estate, a part that can be mastered in only a few trips. The "how to" chapters of this book will give you a good foundation, but you'll have to take this knowledge and make it work for you.

LEVERAGE

All of the reasons why real estate is such a good area for spending your time and money are enhanced by the law of leverage. Leverage means making a little do a lot. If you can buy an $180,000 property that has the potential of being a $220,000 property with a few thousand dollars of fix up, and only put a few thousand dollars down, it's a great deal. You're making a little do a lot.

Most investors are satisfied with a ten percent leverage factor. While many pay that much from time to time, four percent and five percent down payments are not uncommon.

Let's think about this for a minute. If you can pick up a really good deal for only five percent down, what does that mean? Let's say you get an $180,000 property for $9,000 in back payments. The down payment comes out to five percent of $180,000; but what if the property is worth $220,000? Our $9,000 is only three percent of that amount. This is a great area to see leverage working at its best.

How close to reality are these figures? I'm amazed at my own deals, but as I teach about foreclosures around the country and hear about the terms people are picking up, I'm astonished. The closer to the beginning of the time line that you get involved, the better the deal.

I have purchased many types of properties, many different ways, but I've never found any that compared with the beautiful leverage found with purchasing foreclosures. Specifically, my average down payment (back payments and foreclosure costs) totaled about five percent of the actual costs and about four percent of the estimated market value.

This is good news. There are many people with the time and the fortitude it takes to locate and process a property, but with this leverage factor in mind, purchasing foreclosures solves the big problem of large down payments.

PRICES ARE LOWER

It's hard to bring up the obvious, but if I'm going to do a complete job with this book, I need to mention the pricing advantage of picking up foreclosures.

You'll see the cautions about determining value in another chapter and you'll read about the effects of inflation in yet another, but when you actually climb in the ring you are going to find many foreclosures that are sitting good deals.

Some will need very little clean up. Some will only be a few payments behind. And, some will have anxious owners ready to unload them immediately. I know this won't happen often, but it will happen. These properties are nice, and even if it takes more time, energy and money in these different areas, it will most likely be well worth it.

I have no ready formulas but I know from experience that, whatever the case, most of these properties are tremendous deals in terms of price. All the forces of the market place are working to help the property increase in value. And, in most cases, the homeowner has done his share to help. Very seldom have I seen a property deteriorate faster than upward inflation. All of this leaves the property sitting there waiting for someone to see its potential. You'll develop a good eye for finding this potential and these good deals will be yours.

FREE AND CLEAR

This section could have been placed in the chapter on the auction block because this situation only happens with properties that make it to the auction sale. It's important here, though, because this is the chapter on dreams.

Once the property has passed along the time line and is actually sold at auction, all the liens except the one being foreclosed on (usually a first mortgage of some sort) will be removed.

If the purchase price had been $125,800 to satisfy the first mortgage all other private liens would be abolished. You would get a deed to the property free and clear and not one other lien holder would have recourse against you.

NOTE: public liens such as property taxes, assessments, IRS and public utility liens stick with the property.

NOTE: this is only at the actual foreclosure sale. If you, as an investor, purchase the property anytime before the sale, you will be getting it for just the back payments, but you will also be assuming any other current liabilities. That is why it is essential

(TITLE)

that you do a check of the tile status before allowing the property to be deeded to you.

YOUR FRIENDLY BANKER

Most of you who are familiar with my other books know that I'm not too fond of banks. I won't belabor that point here, but I want you to realize that I'm not singing a different song with the following information.

Not only has the current economic crisis affected people, it has also affected banks. For the past few years banks have played the tough guys, but until something changes, Simon Lagree has been tamed.

Oh, some will still call everything due and play the bad guys. Some have to do this for their economic survival. They need the loans repaid to pay the telephone bill. But there are plenty of them holding properties that they would love to sell. (See the chapter on finding properties for information on processing these properties). Banks need to unload these properties because it makes their books look bad. You see, banks are continually being rated by state and federal authorities. This is a grading system that allows "good" banks certain freedoms to make different types of loans.

If their books look bad, then they may be severely restricted. Talk about percentages-believe it or not, they have ratios and formulas even the bankers get tired of.

AN INVESTOR'S DREAM

Once banks take a property back, it shows up on their financial statement as REO (Real Estate Owned). That may sound good, but it shows up in the liability section, as there is no outstanding receivable loan to offset it. Too many of these showings looks bad. Now it's time to help them out-offer to take several off their hands.

ALL TERMS ARE NEGOTIABLE. You'll discover quickly who is willing to work with you. You have no time for nerds (I've always wanted to use that word in one of my books, but it didn't seem appropriate until now.) Remember, you are helping them as much or more than they are helping you. Helping them may help your dream come true YOUR REAL ESTATE MONEY MACHINE.

Have you ever wished that investing in real estate could be run like a business? Or wished that procedures could be established once and then work continually? On that processing properties had a beginning, middle and end? And that everything could be more organized, where good deals were not found only by "stumbling" onto them? The last section of this dream chapter concerns processing foreclosures as a business. Almost all other aspects of investing in real estate involve a hit and miss, "get it if you're there," approach. Not so with foreclosures. They are always there, even in the best of times. Once you have the questions answered on the questionnaire included in this book, and understand how to wedge yourself into the time line, you are on the road to a systematic approach that works the same everyday. As a matter of fact, if it weren't for the different personalities that you'll meet, processing these properties could get boring. You could even get it down so well that you could work it 9 to 5 with normal holidays off.

Doesn't that sound nice? Picking up great deals with low down payments, helping people save their credit rating, and still being able to get home in time for your favorite TV program! This has been my goal from the beginning to create a machine that would spin off a perpetual monthly income and leave my time free. Processing foreclosure properties was a big boon to that goal.

SUMMARY

Most of us, as investors, have certain things that we want out of any investment plan. All of the reasons mentioned in this chapter point to foreclosures as an excellent avenue.

Even if it doesn't become a full-time "business" for you, understanding the ins and outs of this system will help you spot good deals. After all, even one good deal would bring in an extra $20,000 or so this month. Not too bad for some of us smaller investors.

QUESTIONNAIRE

The questionnaire on the following pages is to help you zero in on the process in your individual state. It will take some research to sift through all of this and come up with answers that are functional as well as right. I would have saved a lot of time had I known these questions when I started picking up foreclosures. This form is a basic place to start. Use your intuition to pick up on other items that may be important. If the information you find frightens you, let it sit for a few days and come into perspective.

QUESTIONNAIRE

Person talked to_____

Phone #_____Phone #_____

State_____

State general conditions of the foreclosure process_____

_____

_____

_____

_____

How long before the sale (auction) may the property be cured?

_____

What are some of the things needing to be done to cure the loan?

_____

_____

_____

_____

_____

_____

_____

What are the expenses involved in curing the loan?

_____

_____

_____

What are the differences between a sheriff's sale and a trustee's sale?

_____

_____

_____

What is the situation with Due-on-Sale clauses?

_____

_____

_____

What liens will be eliminated at the auction?

_____

_____

_____

What types of liens are not affected?

_____

_____

_____

What rights does the homeowner have?

_____

_____

_____

How long does he have to exercise these rights?

_____

_____

_____

What other state laws (or court cases) have to be contended with?

1._____

_____

_____

2._____

_____

_____

3._____

_____

_____

How long after the auction before possession?

_____

_____

_____

What steps must be taken during this time?

1._____

_____

_____

2._____

_____

_____

3._____

_____

_____

What are some exceptions that will help?

_____

_____

_____

May the actual deliverance of the money at the auction be delayed?_____ How long?_____

_____

How much is needed right then?

_____

_____

Other Points

_____

_____

_____

_____

_____

Can you tell me anything else that I may need to know to avoid problems or speed up the process?

_____

_____

_____

_____

_____

_____

_____

_____

RECORD KEEPING

Let me show you how I keep track of processing these properties. This system will deviate from my standard record keeping system. Because of its uniqueness, foreclosures need a special system.

I may be processing 10 to 15 different properties at one time. In order to keep my thinking straight and make sure that no information is lost, I use one, regular, 3-ring binder, one inch thick, with dividers (thick paper or card stock) to separate each property. Use the form on the next page. You may make copies of this and use one per property. If you need additional space use a blank sheet. This is recommended anyway as you can cut out the announcement and tape or glue it to the separate sheet.

NOTE: the reason it says "possible foreclosure" is because it's just that--a possibility. If anyone sees this page (especially the home-owner) that is how he views it a possibility. Be careful of writing "FORECLOSURES" on the outside of the binder.

POSSIBLE FORECLOSURE

Address of Property_____

_____

_____

Trustee (or individual) handling sale

_____ Phone # _____

Owner of Property_____

Phone #_____Phone #_____

Reason for Action _____

_____

_____

_____

Is home vacant? Yes_____ No _____

If yes, has owner been located? Yes_____ No _____

Means used to try and locate forwarding address:

_____letter,_____ phone listings, _____neighbors

Information on above:

_____

_____

_____

Sale Date_____

Date to Stop Sale (Cure) _____

Estimated Market Value _____

Loan Balance _____

Other Loans or Liens _____

Total of Loans _____

Estimated Fix Up Costs _____

Total Costs (Loans and Fix Up) _____

Estimated Net Gain _____

The weakest ink is better than the best memory. Take copious notes. It's so important to have all the information you've gathered available to you in an easy-to-understand format. If some of the forms and questionnaires in this book aren't functional for you, make up some that are. Get YOUR system down pat. You'll be running so fast and furious while tracking down the property and the people, that it's easy to forget to keep notes and thoughts. If you fail to do so, it will hinder your decision making progress.

But just think what it will be like if your forms and questionnaires are filled out properly and completely. If you, perchance, have a meeting with your investment counselor, an attorney or a CPA, his job will be easier with complete information.

It is important to write things down.

Chapter 5

How To Find Properties

" PEOPLE USUALLY MOVE WITHIN THE SAME
LARGE CITY OR SURROUNDING SMALL TOWNS."

Chapter 5

How To Find Properties

There are many ways to find foreclosure properties. If you have determined from Chapter I where you want to fit in on the time line, you'll then have to pick from the following list, the ways you want to get involved.

PUBLIC ANNOUNCEMENTS

It obviously comes down to you and how much energy you want to expend finding this type of property. Foreclosures are available in all stages of the time line. If you want to do minimal work, then the best place to find properties is in the public announcements, so we'll talk about those first. But, if you want to do more work, then read on through the rest of this chapter and you'll see several different alternatives for finding the properties before it gets close to the cure date.

There are two places public announcements can be found. The first place is in the local newspaper. If you'll look near or in the classified section, you'll see notices for trustee's or sheriff sales. We'll differentiate between these two sales at a later point. For our purposes, look for any kind of trustee sale, and if your state has sheriffs sales, where the sheriff represents the trustee or bank, then you'd be looking for those kinds of sales. You're looking to find properties which are being foreclosed on because of nonpayment of a mortgage or some type of loan. These are mortgage foreclosures.

The other place to find foreclosures is the legal records for your city. Most cities over 100,000 have such legal publications. These papers include everything that occurs in the county and are usually published daily. Some smaller cities might have theirs published twice a week. These will include every bankruptcy, every business license, every bid for government job, every divorce and marriage; all legal notices filed against people and their properties are there.

With this type of legal journal in hand, you will learn to recognize the good deals. These are your main avenues to finding properties that have reached the final and serious stages of foreclosure.

ATTORNEYS

Another good place to find properties is through the attorneys who are trustees for the banks. Not too many attorneys handle these types of problems. In a city of 200,000 to 500,000 people, there are probably 10 to 15 trustee attorneys. They represent banks, mortgage companies, or saving and loans, and do nothing but process these loans.

Dealing with these attorneys is very tricky and taxing in that most of them act like attorneys. They believe that they have some kind of information which they can hide.

Even though there are only a limited number of attorneys who deal with foreclosures, even these attorneys do not do this full time. This is just a part of their business. They don't like to spend a lot of time doing this because it's very negative and draining to deal with people in these situations. It's difficult to get in touch with people, and they have to write nasty letters trying to get payments.

I have sometimes been able to sweet-talk an attorney, but only if he understood that I was going to be able to take some problems off his hands. I've even offered to pay attorneys money to help me process some of these deals (which was rejected because they would then be representing two parties).

As we talked about one deal, I would casually mention that I had the funds available to pick up five or six other deals, and wonder whether they would be willing to let me know about some of the other foreclosures they were processing. Some of them were very anxious to give me the names and addresses of people who were losing their houses, even ones who were in the early stages of foreclosure. Some of them would not do that. They would tell me to just wait until the information came out in the notices.

Inform them that you can wait, but pry and dig any way you possibly can. Some attorneys will work with you and some simply won't. However, if they understand that you're not trying to take advantage of people, but are trying to help them and save their credit ratings, and that you'll take over these houses and get them fixed up so the banks they're representing will get their money on time (because you are a good investor), many of them will be more than willing to help you with the new deals. While you're tracking down one property, make it a point to keep asking attorneys about other properties.

If you don't know who these attorneys are, they may be listed by categories in your local yellow pages. Another way is to ask any attorney you know if he knows of any attorneys who process foreclosures. Another source would be to go through your daily legal journal or newspaper, and see the names that are there. You'll probably see certain names coming up consistently. Those are the attorneys to call.

Any attorney can process a foreclosure. But I've found in the past that most attorneys specialize, and that one attorney may work for five or six of the largest savings and loans (or other banks) in the state. There may be one legal office that handles all of the foreclosure action for these institutions. To find out the attorneys who are processing these properties, just call the office or bank and ask them.

Try to schedule a meeting with them to show them what you're attempting to do. I have found that even though I've been able to make good friends with some of these attorneys on the phone, it has been very tough to arrange a meeting with them. If there is any other reason for having lunch with them (such as any other legal problems that you may be having), use it. Then tell them that you plan to pick up several houses on foreclosure and wonder if they know of any. If it's at all possible, rather than call an attorney on the phone, go to the office and talk to the secretary who is handling the foreclosures.

I ask the secretary if I can see the attorney for just a couple of minutes to ask him some questions about the foreclosure. It is usually very hard to get through the secretary, but if I can, it is very beneficial, and usually I am not charged for this time.

The attorneys are paid by the bank to process these properties. You might even remind him that one of the purposes of the legal notice is to solve this problem for the homeowner.

These attorneys are acquainted with each other. Once an attorney informed me that a certain large mortgage company just turned over 120 of these properties. He had so many to process that he wanted anyone to take them off his hands. Once you know about the property, all you need is the address and the name of the people, and you can go to town processing the foreclosure.

REAL ESTATE AGENTS

I have found in the past that working with real estate agents on these foreclosures has been a very pleasurable experience. Most real estate agents are very empathic to the plight of the people involved. They understand the problems. They, themselves, have possibly been in the cash-short position before.

The reason real estate agents know about foreclosures is because people who are in trouble generally hire a real estate agency to sell the house for them.

Most people are very honest with real estate agents and explain to them that they are four payments behind and need to get the house sold right away or they will lose it. The agent knows that if he sells the house within the time frame, he will not only make money on it, but will be able to help this person. If he does not sell the house in the time frame, the person will lose the house and he will not get any commission from it.

For these reasons, most real estate agents realize the urgency of the matter. In any profession, there are going to be the good and the bad, but luckily the last few years of hard times has weeded out most of the bad from the real estate profession. The quality of real estate agents has increased because only the good ones have made it. They are usually those who were empathic and went to bat for the people. They are the ones who went the second mile. Good real estate agents are willing to entertain new ideas, but because the agent is representing the seller, the property is probably up somewhere near its full market value (especially, if all of the work and other repairs are done to the property, to prepare it for the sale).

You are trying to buy the properties as is—with all of its latent and patent defects. Even though the properties are there, these might not be the best deals for you as the investor because you need to find the really good deals.

The following story actually happened. I wish it had not happened. It happened at a time when there was a glut of real estate agents. Most of them were making money sitting around their offices with their feet up on their desks, and not really working very hard.

I came across an agent who had a property listed which I knew beforehand was in foreclosure. I tracked it down through the ads as always, but when I arrived at the vacant property, I saw a real estate sign in front of it. Rather than try to track it down through the owner and get the property through him, I went ahead and called the real estate agent. The agent met me there and showed me through the property. I was very interested in it.

Fixed up, the property was probably worth $5,000 to $6,000 more than what the loan balance was. The person bought the property with hardly anything down a few years before. It had not appreciated in value much; it was in a run-down condition with many windows broken. The whole yard needed landscaping.

Because of the amount of work that needed to be done, I offered to take over the back payments which totaled about $2,000 and pay the man $500. I would also pay the real estate agent $500. The real estate agent looked at me like I was crazy and said that he would not present such an offer. I told him he needed to present this offer, that it was his legal obligation to present this offer, and he still refused to do it. It was a good offer in view of the fact that it was only one day before the cure date and this man was going to lose the property.

The next day I went to the real estate agent's office and spoke with the broker. He heard the offer, said it was not that bad, did not understand his agent's reluctance, but he was too busy that day to present the offer.

The agent was not in and probably would not present the offer anyway. The next day at the cure date, I went back to the office to see if the offer had been presented. It had not. I stood there not only furious over the fact that I had lost out and spent a lot of time tracking down this house, but the man was losing out on getting $500, and his credit rating was now ruined for the next seven years.

I stood there until both the agent and the broker were free. I went into their office and said, "I do not understand what you have done. I do not understand why you did not make the offer to this man. The man lost his house at 10:00 this morning. I do not particularly care about you right now because of what you have just done to me and what you have just done to this man, so I do not care about your commission. But, I do not understand why you would forego losing out on $500 worth of commission. It seems that $500 is better than nothing." The agent had the audacity to stand there and look me in the eyes and say he would never present an offer like the one I wanted presented.

I was totally shaken by that kind of comment, to realize that somebody with a character that low had passed the tests and become an agent. I looked at him and said, "You do not like what I was offering, to pay the man $500 and save him from foreclosure. Is what you just did to the man any better than what I was offering him?" He stared back at me. I continued by suggesting that we have a meeting as soon as it could be arranged between that man, the broker, the agent and the board of complaints at the local real estate board office.

At that point, the agent started to realize that his license was on the line. I stated that I felt he had no right working in the real estate field. "You have just done a man more disservice than I have ever seen done before. If I were you, I would just hang up my license. As a matter of fact, I am going to walk away from this one because I do not have time to deal with you. I am not going to get up on a white horse right now. You have messed up your client, and if I ever see you working in real estate again, I will proceed to process this complaint."

That was as much of a white horse or soapbox as I wanted to get onto that day. However, it made me realize that even though most real estate agents are working in the best way for their clients, some are not.

You and I, as investors, need to realize that when an offer is made on a house, it is their obligation to present it. Even if your offer may seem ridiculous to them, it is not up to them to decide.

Chapter 6

Step By Step

Chapter 6

Step By Step

It is the purpose of this chapter to lay out the process for following through with the acquisition of foreclosures. Let's make the assumption that you've found the property in a legal notice. Your appetite is whetted with the information you've read and you're ready to start tracking it down.

SEVEN BASIC STEPS

There are seven basic steps to follow. There are also several helpful hints for specific property types, and for making the plan work in a general sense. These hints, notes, and cautions will be included as we go along.

One more thing, many of these steps will happen within a day. Even though this is an A to Z, step-by-step process, with the steps listed in order of importance, it's good to get the ball rolling on all fronts. For example, if you've called the attorney and are waiting for a call back (and the whole deal still looks good), don't hesitate to check the title. You may, out of necessity, find it mandatory that you process the property from all angles. If you don't, someone else might.

Note, Hint, Caution #1: look at the date of the mortgage. This should be a special area of concern. Unusual financing arrangements or high interest rates have caused many properties to have inordinately high monthly payments. This is probably the number one contributing factor to why the property is being foreclosed on.

How To Read The Ad

Look at the parties involved. Does it look like a single family residence?

What is the date of the Mortgage or Deed or Trust?

What Date is the auction scheduled for?

What is the cure date? Is this cure date listed or are you relying on your state laws for this information?

Is the common (street) address included?

Is any of the loan information listed?

Who do you contact to process the sale?

Also, new loans have extremely restrictive clauses which make the properties not only hard to assume now, but also make them hard to dispose of later. The banks have painted themselves into an awful corner. It's really a no-win situation, but some will still go all out and act on each of the restrictive provisions of their documents.

These two items should make you very cautious of loans that were taken out in the 1980s. Pre-1979 loans are generally good. That's about the time the interest rates (and monthly payments) went so high. The aftershock of the increased interest rates was a change in the terminology in the bank's favor.

I'm stating this in a general sense. You'll never really know what the terms are like until you call. And once you call, you're in the right spot to find out what the bank is doing with these foreclosures. Don't take anything for granted. They may be amenable to any offer. Also, they change their minds and procedures all the time. When they have their management meetings they will make new decisions. They will, in effect, float with whatever seems best at any given time.

One more item—FHA and VA loans are excellent to process. Along with the property, special note should be given to the terms of the loans. In this case though, all you should be concerned with is the amount of the monthly payment. These loans are assumable, which is good because all of your selling options

By the way, the VA did make some changes on assumptions. A new buyer, non-veteran, may now fully assume the loan and release the previous owner (veteran) from future liability and free up all his eligibility amounts for processing future loans. Check with your bank or the Veterans Administration for details.

Note, Hint, Caution #2: we've covered the time line extensively, but now, as you're looking at the announcement, it's time to find out all the dates involved so you know how much time you have.

The major concern of processing these properties is to get them tied up before the cure date. It can be done in a few days if everything goes like clockwork, but the whole process takes up to a week.

Where on the time line do you fit in? Can you make it before the cure date? A few phone calls will answer this last question.

STEP #1- LOOK AT THE PROPERTY

Do not use up any of your time processing the legal work until you've seen the property. Until you do that, you don't know what the neighborhood looks like. You don't know if it's vacant or not, and, you don't know what condition it is in. If you don't know these things you never know how much you'll make, so you won't know how much money to risk.

Note, Hint, Caution #3: now that you've seen the property, you can determine if you'll need help in appraising it. If you're good at this, then fill in the form and move on. But if you aren't quite sure, then get someone else to help you. This person could be an appraiser, realtor, or another investor with more experience. If you're in a hurry, I suggest the latter.

Note, Hint, Caution #4: you still don't know enough to make a proper decision until you've done Step 4 which is to check the title. You'll need to find out if there are other liens or encumbrances that will alter how much equity you're dealing with.

Note, Hint, Caution #5: you really need to see the inside if you are to properly make the decision. This is extremely difficult sometimes. If you can't get in, your options are to:

1. Walk away and look elsewhere
2. Keep trying
3. Go ahead on your feelings that it is still okay

You have one thing that makes the determination of the value easier. In most cases, the way people keep up the outside of their houses is just about how they keep up the inside. Of course, there are exceptions, but I've never been too disappointed if I trusted the condition of the outside.

Note, Hint, Caution #6: what happens if the announcement only contains the legal description? That presents a small problem, but it can be solved by one of the following:

1. Call or go to the title company and look up the common or street address
2. Go to the courthouse and look it up
3. Call the attorney (trustee or sheriff) and ask for it

STEP #2 - CALL THE TRUSTEE

Now that you've seen the property, it's time to start gathering the information needed to make the decision, and finalize the current procedure that this particular trustee will use.

You start by making a phone call. Don't feel bad if you don't get all of the information you need right away. Your goal is to finish filling out the questionnaire, but it is frustrating because you'll get the secretary whose job it is to handle as much as possible. She'll know some of what you need to find out, but, unless she's really got her act together, she will not be able to tell you exactly what you need to do to stop the foreclosure.

Note, Hint, Caution #7: many times the announcement has a lot of information about the amounts needed to cure the loan, BUT THIS INFORMATION IS NOT CURRENT. The trustee puts the announcement in the paper several weeks before the actual sale. The information may be current at the time the ad is placed, but as the foreclosure moves along the time line, the expenses continue to mount.

You need to find out the exact amount that it will take to cure it now. And that even needs to be expanded upon. You are probably not ready yet to cure it the day that you're making this call. If it takes you a few more days to wrap up the other things that need to be completed, the expenses might increase yet again.

Let's put this into context. You read the announcement and calculate from the information given that it will take about $2,000 to cure the loan. You have that amount and you also have about $1,000 which you'll need to fix it up. (You can sometimes calculate the monthly payments in arrears just by counting forward from the date given to the present.)

After talking to the attorney, you realize that it will take $2,800 to cure the loan-not $2,000. Now it's decision time once again. Let's not go into that, except to say that in most cases the deal will be right-right enough to try to secure additional funds or do less with the property in terms of fix up, etc. The point is made, be careful about the accuracy of the information in the ad.

Back to the phone conversation. Sometimes the only way that I've been able to get through to the decision maker (if it's necessary) is to keep asking questions until the secretary runs out of answers. She will gladly try to help by letting you through to her boss.

I've dropped by the attorney's office at times when I thought the property justified it, which put an obligation on the attorney to see me. They can always squeeze in one more.

It is helpful to be pleasant to the person at the front desk, because it is her job to shield the boss from "unimportant" matters. This kindness has opened many doors for me. And, I know, from sad experience, how quickly the doors close when I get frustrated with their apathy and impertinence.

If you are going to proceed and process this property, this phone call will just be the first of many. Try to get all the information you need to pursue the deal during this first phone call. Calling back right away for more information will be a stumbling block in the peace process.

Note, Hint, Caution #8: it may seem that I'm coming down pretty hard on the trustees or people processing foreclosures, especially attorneys. I don't mean to be rude to them, but my experience tells me that they are sometimes arrogant and not willing to help. I think I know why this is. Most of them hate going through with the sale as it's boring and embarrassing. But, most of them are tired of being annoyed with dealing with the old homeowner and then dealing with several "looky-loo's" (people who look and look and never move to action).

STEP #3 - CHECK WITH THE BANK

It is now time to put the finishing touches on the information gathering system. Go to the bank and check into the following:

1. The exact loan balance
2. The exact monthly payments and will there be any changes
3. The legal documents that you will be signing

It is important that you find out anything and everything you can about the bank's position on the property. This is not an area where you will want to have surprises.

STEP #4 - GET A TITLE REPORT

Go to a title company or to the courthouse and look closely at the title status of the property. Also, check the person's name to see if there is anything against him that might cause a problem when he conveys it. You will want to look at the fine print of any documents that will affect you. You could also inform them of what you are doing and start the process for acquiring title insurance.

STEP #5 - CONTACT THE HOMEOWNER

It is now time to contact the homeowner. Before I tell you how to find him, if he is not living in the house, let us discuss why you need him.

There are only a few ways of changing ownership of property from one person to another. One way is for some government entity to sign it over. There are many ways they do this, but for our purposes here, the only ones we are concerned with are the sheriff's sale and some kind of foreclosure court.

The other way is for the homeowner to sign the deed himself. This deed needs to be signed by the parties that have the legal right to convey the property. For example, a husband and wife may have bought the property, but the wife ended up with the property after a divorce. She has sole title to the property. She alone can then deed the property. Whoever stands in the chain of title now is the one that you will need to have sign the deed.

Usually the homeowner is long gone. Here are several ways to locate him.

1. Go to the post office and pay one dollar for a change of address update. You will have to have a reason. Tell the clerk that you want to stop the guy's house from going into foreclosure.

Note, Hint, Caution #9: do this right away, even if you are trying other angles. They may fall through. This takes a few days, so it needs to be started quickly.

2. Check with the neighbors for any information about the people. This will be a good time to ask about the property.
3. Check with the bank or the trustee to see if they know the owner's current address or phone number.
4. Most people move out, but they move close by. Call telephone directory assistance and ask.

    Make sure you try all possible names that they could be listed under. One time I found eight people with the same name. I had to call all of them. One time there were six, but the operator told me which one was a new listing. It was the right one.

5. Send the people a letter through the old address. If they are not having their mail forwarded, they or someone they know is probably checking their mail box.

6. See if anyone knows who their relatives are. Maybe the neighbors can help out. All I can say is this-nothing can happen until they are found. Pull out all the stops.

STEP #6 - HAVE HOMEOWNER SIGN THE DEED

Any simple quit claim deed will do. Get one from the title company or an office supply store. Remember his, her or their signature(s) must be notarized. Do this properly so there will be no problems.

STEP #7 - CONTACT THE BANK AND THE TRUSTEE TO FINISH

Hopefully, the bank and the trustee will not be out in the cold as you have been doing all this. They should know that you are coming.

Once you have all the proper forms signed, take them to the attorney (or whoever is handling the case), with a cashier's check for the amount needed to cure it. They have nothing to do but accept it. The property is already yours. You have a deed with your name on it. Ask if there is anything else and if not, leave and go have a party.

Chapter 7

How To Value The Property

TAKE THE UNCERTAINTIES OUT
OF THEIR LIVES.

Chapter 7

How To Value The Property

I have a favor to ask of you, the reader. This chapter may look like an easy one to skip over, but I ask that you do not. Processing foreclosures has its own system. You are dealing with time and time passes very quickly. I'll mention several ways that are common when talking about evaluating a property, but there are a few special ones that will aid you, especially, if you need to act quickly. At the end of this chapter, I'll end with an unusual twist to evaluating each and every property, so I encourage you to read it thoroughly.

Using the form included in this book for record keeping, you can list your basic feelings about the market value of the property and the amount of money needed to fix it up. Once you know the loan balances, you are prepared to make your decision as to whether you should buy the property or not. This sounds so simple, but doing it is not simple at all. Probably the single greatest fear I encounter as I travel around the country speaking and consulting, is the fear of paying too much for a property. Put in its proper perspective, this is a good fear to have because it makes one cautious. It causes people to look twice.

This chapter will list several procedures for helping you evaluate the value of the property. Use these procedures in con-junction with each other. Don't put all your eggs in one basket.

OPINIONS

Most of these procedures involve other people's opinions. That's okay if they are qualified. There are two basic ways to determine values:

1. What did it cost to build, but more importantly, what would it cost to replace?
2. Comparably. What have similar houses sold for in the same area?

You'll quickly realize how difficult it is to determine either of these, but there are, some established systems that are not too far off base.

THE APPRAISAL

You can hire someone to come out and give you an appraisal. This appraisal has many varieties. It all depends on what you want it to do.

- It could be done to establish the value, independently of what you are thinking.
- It could be done to verify your opinion.

An **MAI *or other professional appraisal*** is the top of the line. They take into account everything. It takes a little longer and costs a lot more, but if you need to know what a property is worth, this type of appraisal will get it down to the penny. There are two other things to consider with this type of appraisal:

1. They may even tell you what the property will be worth all fixed up. This obviously becomes very difficult as they don't know exactly how you'll fix it up (what quality of

materials or, workmanship you'll use), but you may get a professional ball-park figure.

2. If the money you're using to process or fix up the property is coming from a lending institution this may be the only type of appraisal that they will accept.

An *FHA* Appraisal is probably the most conservative appraisal on the market. You don't have to be buying or selling the house FHA to have one done. Just call their office and order it. The cost should be under $150 and could take a few weeks. You'll need to consider this time period. If the property looks good to you from a set of figures determined from other sources you may want to get this FHA appraisal anyway, so you'll have it to:

1. Tell you what needs fixing up in order to sell it FHA. Remember, in good times this is the most common type of financing.
2. Show your banker or prospective purchasers. Once any work is completed you can have the appraisal updated.
3. Base your decisions on it. Wouldn't it be nice just to have it so you can better determine the direction you'll take with the property?

If you're in a hurry you may need to have other investors look at the property for you. It's nice to have friends who can give you some feedback on a moment's notice. It would be best if these people do not have a personal interest in the property except to help you out.

It would also be best if there is some disagreement about the different aspects of the property. Why? Because decisions based on a foundation of conflicting opinions stand a better chance of being right. Don't look for "yes" people. It's nice to have positive feedback and encouragement, but it's also nice to have someone throw a bucket of cold water on you once in a while. Don't over-look the value of these people's opinions. They may have exten-sive experience in investing, experience that could fill the gaps for you.

Many real estate agents would be glad to help. If they have expe-rience or access to comparables or other information this could be a valuable service to you.

CHECK YOURSELF

You can do a lot on your own. You can call and ask the price of other properties in the neighborhood. You could talk to neigh-bors, et cetera. Remember though, that this information is high-ly subjective. It needs to be scrutinized closely.

You will develop your own level of expertise in this area. Common sense will tell you much. It took a lot for me to learn to trust my own feelings, but it became my best meter. I could put on paper all the pros and cons, list the values that I thought appropriate, and then list my options. I could then sit back and let my fears and excitement determine if it was right for me.

One other thing—I have a time line also. At different points in time purchasing, a given property may not be right. It could have been right two weeks before, but now is not the time. The value of the property to you is also determined by how much time, ener-gy and availability of money that you have at any given time.

A FEW OTHERS

There are a few other ways to determine value, but even though you can get good at these, they are subjective to the point of almost requiring backup opinions and procedures. They will, however, get you in the ball park and should be considered. These procedures include:

1. Looking at the tax rolls. If you can determine what percentages of assessed value your local tax auditor uses, and add to this figure the increased amount due to inflation, you should be close to the current value.
   Note, Hint, Caution: hopefully, you'll see the flaws of using this as the only procedure. So many other factors have to be taken into consideration.
2. Look at the legal documents. Most often you will be able to tell what the previous owners paid for the place. The same cautions apply as in number 1 above.
3. The bank or the trustee (attorney) may have obtained an appraisal, so they know what they are dealing with. They usually do, but they may be reluctant to let you have access to it. Be persistent and assure them that it's in their best interest.

FIX-UP

Before you get too far into the process, it would be good to determine how much it will take to repair the property and put it into whatever shape you have determined. Once again, your own experience can tell you a lot about these costs, but you can also get subcontractors to come and give you bids. You can then use this information to help fill in the form.

MARKETABILITY

Before we end this chapter, let's consider one final aspect. The aspect of the marketability of the property. We can analyze the features and costs of the property until we turn blue, but we should consider the following:

If we want to sell:
1. What can we sell it for?
2. How long will it take to sell?
3. What will we do to cover costs in the meantime?

If we want to rent:
1. Can we rent it?
2. What will it rent for?

The worst kind of alligator is one with no income and no readily available way to dispose of it. The determination should not be that difficult, but it needs to be done.

SUMMARY

These are just some procedures for determining value. Once completed, you'll have to combine any information received with your own thinking. If ever in doubt, use several ways to determine present and future value and fix up costs. It will never hurt to do more than is necessary in this regard.

And now, I'll explain the different twist to the importance of getting a good evaluation on each property. You have spent a lot of time being concerned with the time line. You have fretted and sweated over getting things done on time. If you've moved quickly and properly, the property is now yours.

Now the property needs to fit into your time line, into your game plan. So many options will now open up to you that you'll need the proper foundation that you've created to assure continued intelligent actions.

Appraising the value of the property is important, but appraising your total situation is more important. The entrance to the right road starts by doing the right things.

Chapter 8

Things To Avoid

 **SAME**

 **WORSE**

BETTER

Chapter 8

Things To Avoid

You'll obviously want to run this investment strategy with as few hitches as possible, but like everything else, picking up foreclosures also has some caution zones.

If you've already looked at foreclosures and even tested the water, you'll know several of these. I learned about these "red flag" areas after looking at, and processing, several properties. I only wished at that time that I could have read a book like this to tell me what to watch out for. Hopefully, you will be able to avoid these time-consuming delays that constantly hampered me.

OTHER LIENS

The first caution is other encumbrances that exist against the title to the property. It would be easy to just talk about second mortgages, but the problem is more extensive than that. There are numerous ways that a property owner could have liens put against the property. Some might be involuntary, but to compound the matter, the owner might not even know about certain liens or encumbrances against him or the property.

Once again, let's turn to the time line. If you're processing the property before the cure date and you get a deed signed by the owner, you will inherit any and all of his problems, including any liens or judgments. These liens could show up against the property, but they could also show up against his name. If a proper title check (and/or report) is done, all of these will be discovered and taken into consideration. After they show up you'll be able to make decisions on how to deal with them, or whether to deal with them at all.

I surely don't want this to sound ominous. In all of my dealings, only one time did something show up that made the deal impossible to handle. Once in a while small liens show up, and even though my profits would be decreased, they were not large enough to cause termination. As a matter of fact, on most of these properties, the profits were large enough that these liens barely dented it.

Regardless, you should know what you're dealing with. Be cautious and you won't be surprised. These kinds of surprises take all the fun out of investing.

Specifically watch for:
1. Mortgages, contracts or trust deeds (no matter what position they are in).
2. Mechanic liens for work done and not yet paid (these may have been paid but not taken off people are quick to put them on but very lax in erasing them).
3. Assessments from any government agency or improvement district.
4. Tax liens – not only delinquent property taxes, but federal and state liens.
5. Liability judgments (such as an insurance claim or accident suit).
6. Anything else on the title report. If you check for these, then you're on the right track. What you need to know will show up. Don't be caught short by not checking. Order title insurance to protect yourself.

HIDDEN CLAUSES

Once you've checked for any documents standing as a charge against the title of the property, you should examine the "fine print" of the ones you find to ascertain whether there are any restrictions that will hinder your assumption efforts. After all, once the property is deeded to you, you will have to do whatever it takes to get your name on line so you will be responsible. You'll need this full transfer of rights and obligations so you can dispose of the property in any way you see fit.

Be up front with phrases that you don't understand. Go directly to the party involved with the documents and get an explanation. This is also the time to find out the intentions of any lending institution. This is not the time to play games. The lenders or mortgagees of these loans are in this game for keeps. It would be better to walk away than to get tangled up, especially if you'll invest any money at all.

As I travel the country and consult with people, I come across some sad situations. I have found people who dealt improperly with the banks; thinking and hoping that things would change and the problems (restrictions) would disappear, they moved forward. Later, finding themselves in trouble, they want some quick remedy, but, far too often there is nothing that can be done.

There are no secrets. Be up front and deal with these restrictions in the open. With a little practice you'll get good at spotting problems. Remember, 90% of possible problems never happen if dealt with properly.

STRUCTURE, ET CETERA

If you can get into the house, you'll be able to see everything. But, even then you might not be able to check everything, so you'll need to make some allowances. For example, the furnace may be shut off. You may not have the time or the ability to get it operational, but the furnace, like so many other things, is readily fixable.

If it looks okay, then more than likely it will work immediately, or just need a little fix-up. I'll cover more of this in the chapter on establishing values. Let it suffice to say here that the mechanical and structural condition of the property (and the cost to remedy anything) should be a caution area.

RENT CONTROLS

If your goal is to purchase rental units, then take into consideration any and all local and state restrictions. Such controls may dictate how you will hold the property.

TAX WRITE OFFS

Once again, if you plan on the property becoming a rental unit make sure you establish the values of the different types of property you are purchasing (stoves, refrigerators, carpets, drapes, etc.). You'll need this information for tax write offs.

REDEMPTION RIGHTS

I realize these rights are clearly established and if you've completed the questionnaire on page 35, you'll know what they are for your state, but it still concerns me. When I tie up my money

I need to be in control. That means not having to wait for some-one else to act. Someone having a right to redeem (recover) his property scares me so much that I check each time with the legal counsel processing the paperwork to once again establish my rights.

SUMMARY

To put this all in a nutshell: what we're trying to find out is how much the property has and what will eventually represent profit. This is not the place to talk of debt ratios or come up with a magic formula that adds up all the "Xs" and "Ys" to see if there is enough profit before you get to "Z" you'll have to do that yourself and decide if there is enough profit for you to spend your time, energy and money pursuing this house.

One final caution: these transactions have no clones. Similarities, yes, but that's all. Look closely at each property and ask yourself the question that I talk about so much: "What else could one be doing with my time and money?" Then, if all fronts have green lights, proceed as if they were yellow.

Chapter 9

Personal Stories

Chapter 9

Personal Stories

PERSONAL STORY #1

I saw a vacant house and from the outside I could not tell if it had three or four bedrooms. I could not tell whether or not it had a second bathroom. I knew it had a basement, but could not tell if it had a full basement. I finally tracked down the lady, and spoke with her on the phone. I said, "Your house is being foreclosed on, I would like to take it off your hands." She said, "It is yours if you want it, honey."

I arranged to meet her the next day to sign the deed. I went to a bank (to use the notary public) and she didn't show up. I was getting worried. I knew that the house had the potential of selling very quickly for $35,000. I was getting it for $17,000 and for just making up $2,000 back payments. My total was going to be $19,000. 1 really wanted it because this was my first year of investing and this one deal could kick me over the top.

I was just getting ready to leave the bank, when she finally showed up. I asked if she would like any money for the house and she said she didn't. I asked if I could at least pay the $98 closing costs that she paid when she bought it with a VA loan. She agreed. She had lived there for 10 months free. I gave her $98 and she signed all the papers in front of the notary in the bank.

I went to see the house later on in the day. It wasn't a three bed-room house, it was a five bedroom house. It had new kitchen cab-inets, and a full basement. The house was really nice.

There was a little bit of mold on the carpets and walls because of the moisture up in Washington. Moisture sets in when houses are vacant. We cleaned it up a little bit and I sold it right away.

I had some friends that really wanted a house. I called them and said I will sell you this house for $36,000 with $5,000 down. They looked at it and offered me $35,000 with $4,000 down. These are the kind of deals I look for.

PERSONAL STORY #2
There is only one time out of 20 deals that I had somebody quit-claim to me something that was not right. I did the title search and found something against the property that made it impossi-ble for me to get it. I took two people with me as witnesses, went back to their house and ripped up the quitclaim deed in front of them. I had not yet recorded it. I would never record it until I knew exactly where I stood.

PERSONAL STORY #3
There was a beautiful rambler in the suburbs. Although it wasn't well maintained, it had big trees around it and had four or five bedrooms.

The people had a loan at a local finance company for $3,000. The principle owing at this time was $2,000 and the closing costs and interest due made the balance owing about $2,600. They were being foreclosed on for this amount. This is different than a trustee sale in that this loan is in second position. The first loan will have to be assumed. I did a title check by calling the mortgage company. The first mortgage on the house was about $20,000 and the house was worth about $60,000. All I had to come up with was $2,600 to buy this house.

I went to the house frequently to find somebody there, but I never did. I thought for some time that it was vacant, but I found out later that they were both at work and the kids were in school.

I went to the sheriffs sale. These are a little different. I had never been to one before. I gathered up every bit of money I had and took $3,315 with me to the sale. I was standing there with my notebook over my chest so the people wouldn't see my heart pounding. The Sheriff said $2,600. I said $2,650. An elderly lady bid $2,700. I was so scared. Never before had I seen anyone process these houses, and here was this lady bidding against me. When I got up to $3,200, she said $3,250. I said $3,300 and she said $3,310. I said $3,315 – that was all I had. She said $3,320. The Sheriff said going once, going twice, and the house was hers. At Sheriffs sales it is cash in hand at the time of sale with no exceptions.

But wait! The week before I talked to the Sheriff about the process in an effort to learn everything I could about it. The lady whispered something to the Sheriff and left. I asked what was going on and he said she wants some time to go get the money. I said, "You told me it was absolutely cash in hand at time of sale. She can't leave right now." He said, "I suspended the rules this time." I told him he couldn't do that because I could get more money. He said it was too late. I told him it was not too late, I wanted to know his superior. He said that would be the civil officer. I went to talk to him. I explained the whole situation to him. Guess what their solution was? Have another sale the next week! But do you know what would happen? We will both show up next week with more money. It is going to be another fight to see who can gather up the most money. When she came back with the money and the civil officer told her that there would be another sale, she was just furious. I went out to the people's house and I sat there for six hours waiting for them to come home. If I could just get them to quitclaim it to me, then I could make up the $2,600 delinquency. They finally came home. I walked in and talked to the father, and later the mother came in.

They were of German origin and didn't speak English very well. As I was talking to them, they could not believe what was going on. They had never received any notices about this action. They had gone down and taken out a loan when the husband was out of work. The loan was for $3,000. They used their boat and camper as collateral, but the company had gone through and gotten some kind of process and attached it to their house. Then they started foreclosing on their house. No legal notices, no nothing. These people did not know what was going on or what to do now. They had lived in the house for 14 years, had four children and didn't want to lose their house.

I asked if they had an attorney. They said they had a friend that was an attorney. I asked them if he would help them out. They thought he would, so I called him and spent the whole rest of the afternoon telling him what was going on. He saved the house for them the next day.

If there are people living in the house you will have problems because they don't want to leave. It is their house! I am suggesting that if you find vacant houses, go for them. They are good deals, but if there are people living there, consider the alternatives. It is very hard on your heart.

Publisher's Note:

Here is a special offer for those of you who have purchased this book. Wade Cook is now making available a home-study course, *Real Estate Cash Flow System*, complete with an eight cassette tape package, recorded live, along with a student/participant workbook. Wade Cook will give you many ways to buy real estate with little or no cash down! He'll give you reasons why you should invest in real estate, and show how investing in real estate will solve problems, not create them. He will also suggest several ways you can buy with low down payments.

To order call:
Liberty Network, Inc.
1420 NW Gilman Blvd. #2131
Issaquah, Washington 98027
1-866-579-5900

Ask for the Real Estate Cash Flow System. Mastercard or Visa is accepted. Call 1-866-579-5900 and ask for the *Real Estate Cash Flow System.*

Chapter 10

At The Auction

"GOING ONCE, GOING TWICE ... TRUSTEE TAKES POSSESSION."

Chapter 10

At The Auction

If you have large chunks of money or the ability to get it, then this chapter will have a special interest to you. When I say large chunks of money, I mean amounts between $20,000 and $50,000. You will need this in your pocket or in your checking/savings account and not locked away in some promise.

All of the work needed to process and purchase properties before the cure date is much the same work that is needed to buy the property at the auction block. You should have the forms filled out completely. If you feel that the move is right and you have the money, then it is time for you to proceed to the auction. Whoever is handling the sale has the responsibility to see that everyone is treated fairly. Only one time, in all of my trips to these auctions, have I seen anyone else there. So the trustee or the Sheriff is really only protecting the lender. He will go to the courthouse and stand in the main foyer or outside on the main steps and ask for any bids over and above the a) loan balance, b) interest due, and c) foreclosure costs due. If there are no bids, then the bank takes possession of the property and disposes of it in any way it can, IF IT CAN, at new terms.

If someone else bids, then the auction will stop when he stops bidding. Once the trustee has said, "Going once, going twice, sold to the man in the blue shirt," it is yours. There will be a short delay before the property is actually yours. Make sure you follow through and finish the process.

After the bidding, you will have to hand the trustee the money. Different states handle this in various ways.

You may:
- Suspend the sale for an hour or two while you get the cash.
- Put down a deposit (say 10% which will hold the property a day (or even a few days).
- Have to come up with every penny right there.

A few other points to consider:
1. You will be buying the property free and clear.
2. All other liens will be eliminated. This is not so before the cure date, but it is so now.
3. You will have a lot of money tied up and you will need to take special care not to bury short term cash in the property.
4. You should make sure that your cash is buying a lot of excess equity, (or at least the potential is there) over and above the cash you are putting in. Remember, leverage is the key.

These auctions are exciting. They abound in good real estate deals. It just takes some cash and a lot of intestinal fortitude.

Chapter 11

The Effects of Inflation

PICKING UP A FEW FORECLOSURES NOW AND
THEN CAN STRENGTHEN YOUR INVESTMENT PLAN.

Chapter 11

The Effects of Inflation

This might seem like a funny place to be talking about inflation. It's not my intention to delve into anything regarding inflation except how it relates to foreclosures. There are several aspects of foreclosures that become even more interesting once put into the framework of an inflationary setting.

It is too simplistic to say that all property is increasing in value just because of inflationary pressures. After processing several houses, I learned that inflation can have two effects on property; but neither of these two outside inflationary pressures is the key to the direction the property is taking. The real key lies in how the property has been treated by the homeowner.

THE FIRST EFFECT
The first effect of inflation is the help it gives in making the property "maintain" its value. For example, a homeowner can do nothing to fix up his house, and even though it looks more run down than the day he bought it, the market value of the property could be the same or even greater. I have never found a property worth less later than it was when the current homeowner bought it. I am not saying that can't happen, but my experience tells me that people who become homeowners at least try to keep up their houses.

I have come across several houses that looked like they would make that whole last paragraph a lie, but once the surface dirt was gone the real value came through. This is a good point to keep in mind. Once people hit bad times and begin running the risks of losing their house, the first thing they do is let it get messy. They quit doing the little things that keep it nice. I don't know what happens to their thinking (I am not a sociologist), but I do know that a cluttered house and yard is a sign of trouble. If you are looking for clues while out driving around, this could help.

Note: do not be surprised, however, if the people are renters. If they are, this may be an excellent time to contact the owner. He has a problem that you can help him solve.

THE SECOND EFFECT

The most common thing that people do to their property is just maintain it. They will mow the lawn and weed the garden. They will fix a broken toilet or a broken back door; but they won't substantially improve the property. This type of property is more desirable than the ones in the last section in that they have at least kept pace with inflation. For instance, if the house were purchased for $50,000 and inflation has been 10% a year, then two years later the property would be worth a little over $60,000.

It might seem difficult to find well-maintained property going into foreclosure because you would think that if people have kept the place up, surely they have kept up the payments. I tend to agree, but I have noticed that well-kept properties are available.

Sometimes difficulties arise that really set people back. When they do, the house payment seems like the logical item to not pay. After all, money will come from somewhere, and remember, the single largest item of anyone's budget is his house payment. Because it is so large it is the best target for funds. Well-kept houses going into foreclosure are ideal. The money to make up the back payments may be a little larger but the fix-up costs will be quite a bit less.

ONE MORE THING

Before we totally move away from the concept of the prop-erty going up in value, let's cover one more thing. Many people do substantial repairs and improvements on their houses which may really raise the property value. In most cases, these people have enough equity in their properties, and their properties are such that they can be easily resold; thereby solving the owner's problem in a different way.

Don't be surprised if you find a really good deal on a substantially improved house. They will be few and far between, but they are there. The best place to expend your energies is in the lower-priced houses that may look bad.

LOAN PAYOFFS

Another consideration while determining the value of the house is the amount that has been paid of the principal balance owing. The property could have maintained or increased in value, which is good, but the loan balance could also be substantially less. It is simple to check loan balances. Just call the bank or look at the payment record.

ICING ON THE CAKE

From my earliest days of investing I have viewed inflation in a totally different way than most investors. Because it was something that I could not control, I did not want it to be a consideration as to whether purchasing a property was a good investment or not. I just let inflation be the gravy. I want control and there is much that I personally can do to increase the value of the property. So rather than look at an investment that would only be good after waiting a few years, I would look for the good deals right now. With this in mind you can proceed with cautious optimism.

SUMMARY

Stay in control. The force in our lives that causes inflation—deficit government spending—is not likely to go away. The same government that bans cigarette commercials and yet subsidizes the tobacco industry is hardly going to be rational enough or strong enough to curb their debt beast.

Inflation exists and the best way to consider and deal with it is by not basing your investment decisions on it. Let it work for you behind the scenes.

Chapter 12

Other Aspects of Foreclosure

Chapter 12

Other Aspects of Foreclosure

ARE YOU WILLING TO KEEP LEARNING?

There are probably other areas of investing in real estate that will change more rapidly than foreclosures, but processing foreclosures will undergo some radical changes. Why? Because state laws are always changing. Some of the areas of law that change the most are the highly emotional ones. Foreclosures fit the bill, especially when a large number of people feel that the banks are taking advantage of them. The press coverage on these plights is over-whelming.

Don't get me wrong. I think any law that can help people keep their houses has a potential of being a service. I am against government interference in these areas though, and just bring this up so you'll be aware that you will need to keep learning and adapting with the new changes. You'll be a step ahead if you stay on top of these changes and even learn about anticipated changes. Attorneys, banks, and others sometimes know where your state laws are going.

One of the exciting things about real estate is that you can always learn more. The funny thing is that if you take this seriously and invest the proper amount of time in keeping yourself updated and aware, you'll put yourself out in front of other people.

DUE ON SALE CLAUSES

I wish I did not have to bring this up. There is a question on the questionnaire that will help you specify what banks can or cannot do and will or will not do in your state. Often I just walk away. I do not want to be saddled with clauses that would hinder the resale. Use your most persuasive arguments, but realize that you may not be able to budge the banks. Never do anything such as not recording a document in order to fool the banks. That is a game you cannot win, so don't bother playing.

AFTER THE PURCHASE

Now the excitement begins. The house is yours. If you've done your homework, you're left with all of your selling options open. This chapter will not delve into all the ways you can dispose of the property. My other books cover that. I'll just list several things that can be done after the sale.

- Change the locks. You don't know who has a key. You also don't know what kind of mood he might be in.
- Order title insurance to double check what you've just done and get ready for the resale. This will take a while, so get it started right away.
- Write down your options. Give each one a separate page so you can compare later on. Your four basic options are to:

  1. Rent
  2. Sell for Cash
  3. Sell on Contract
  4. Trade

Once you decide the road to take, you can determine how much fixing up to do.

Note, Hint, Caution: it would be wise to start this process long before the property is actually yours.

- Don't let these prospects excite you too much or become too big a disappointment if you don't get them.
- You may come across a new buyer or tenant that could be ready to move in before your paperwork is even finished.

MONEY MACHINE

These are ideal properties for reselling using my quick-turn concept explained in *Real Estate Money Machine*. All the ingredients should be there for a quick resale and building monthly payments. As a matter of fact, if you get really good at finding these, the money machine concept will really aid you because it is a system that will keep up with a large volume of properties.

MULTIPLE UNITS

As you spend time with single family houses, you'll come into contact with multiple family units that are going through the same process. Saying the same process applies may not be wholly accurate because the owner's mentality is a little different and the foreclosure process takes a little longer. This extra time means the amount needed to cure the loan is larger and the desperation of the owner is greater.

This book is not the place to give an extensive look into why these properties are or are not good ones to pick up. Many books are written from the viewpoint of different biases. You've probably read or heard so much on this subject by now that it's boring to you. But, let me add my own opinion here, and then we'll let the matter sit.

Multiple units may be good to pick up if you're accustomed to dealing with them already. If this is not an area of expertise, then sticking with single family houses is probably the best way to go. Consider the following:

1. You really do need to become an expert in some aspect of real estate if you are going to invest in it. Foreclosures are a good area to do this. In dealing with foreclosures, you'll realize that a huge percentage of them are single family houses.
2. Because there are so many houses available, you will develop a wiser use of your time by being where the majority of the market is.
3. When you are ready to sell there is a ready market of buyers. A deal on a multiunit property would have to jump out and knock me down to get me to take it. I know this sounds harsh, but for me, single family houses have all the investment qualities I need.

CONCLUSION

This book has been difficult to write because I wanted to make it national in scope. I have taken special care to point this out repeatedly and encourage you to use the questionnaire as a guide-line. Now that you've read up to here, it's time to fill it in and get going.

I have avoided glaring promises. It would be easy to tell you all the money that I've made or what others have made with foreclosures. You will happily learn this yourself. This area is ripe. The time is right and the deals are there. It just takes somebody with a little gumption. Good luck.

Write me if you have questions or would like to share your successes.

Publisher's Note:

If you would like to be added to our mailing list, please write us at:

Liberty Network, Inc.
1420 NW Gilman Blvd #2131
Issaquah, WA 98024
1-866-579-5900

We will notify you of seminars, presentations, or other exciting events in your area.

Pre-Foreclosures

A note from Wade Cook:

Let me introduce my good friends, Gerald and Paola Romine.
They have perfected a style of investing in foreclosures which
they have graciously made available here.

Pre-Foreclosures

Buying properties in pre-foreclosure can be the most profitable segment of a real estate entrepreneur's business! Unfortunately, it is the most misunderstood. Hopefully, this chapter will shed some much-needed light on the pre-foreclosure subject and how and why you should become involved.

How does the foreclosure process work? When a person buys a house, they normally have a small down payment and obtain a loan from a bank or mortgage broker for the balance of the purchase price. This loan is secured by the property in the form of a mortgage or deed of trust. If the lender does not receive their payments, they may file foreclosure to recover their debt.

The foreclosure process allows the lender to foreclose on any liens or encumbrances in order to take the property and become the legal owner of record, thus allowing the lender to resell the property and recover the original loan amount plus expenses associated with the foreclosure. The foreclosure process can be lengthy depending on the state, but up until the public auction, the homeowner owns the property and has several options available. It's important to realize when talking about pre-foreclosures, we are talking about acquiring the property any time before the public auction sale. The sooner you contact a homeowner in pre-foreclosure, the more time you have to structure a deal and purchase the property.

Many people have the misconception that people buying homes in foreclosure are taking advantage of another person's misfortune. This is simply not true. The lender made a loan in good faith and the borrower agreed to repay the loan. If the borrower does not make the required payments they have broken the agreement and the lender must protect their financial interests and may foreclose on the property as agreed to by all parties when the loan was originally made. Anytime there is a foreclosure, the borrower has broken the terms of the agreement and your involvement solves a problem the homeowner created.

When facing foreclosure, many homeowners bury their heads in the sand hoping it will just go away. No action by the owner ensures a foreclosure, losing the house, a severely damaged credit profile, and a loss of all equity in the home. When dealing with an owner in pre-foreclosure it is important to explain the benefit of avoiding foreclosure if possible:

1. **Protecting Their Credit Profile.** Many times a person in foreclosure is overwhelmed with life-changing events happening and has multiple financial challenges. By working with an investor, it may be possible to stop the foreclosure and start rebuilding their credit profile or prevent their credit profile from getting worse. The foreclosure will come to pass, but in today's credit-conscious society, a credit rating affects everything from buying a car to getting property insurance.
2. **Protect Equity.** When a home is foreclosed all of the equity is lost. By working with an investor it may be possible to recover some of the equity and prevent the foreclosure.
3. **Rebuilding Their Life.** The pressure and strain of a foreclosure effects all area of a person's life. Under such pressure it is not uncommon for people to become depressed,

be unkind to loved ones, or make poor personal and business decisions. Stopping the foreclosure allows a person to remove an albatross from their neck and move on with life.

For the real estate investor there are many ways to financially profit and it can be a great feeling to help people move on with their lives. If not for investors, lenders would foreclose on most properties and the homeowners would lose all equity and have a foreclosure on their records. Investors provide the vital role of helping homeowners salvage some equity, can often help the homeowner's credit, and help people start rebuilding their lives. Unfortunately, may homeowners will not see or understand the vital role investors have, but it is not uncommon to receive thank you letters after stopping foreclosures.

In order for an investor to be involved, there must be a profit, or there is no reason to be involved in the first place. When working with sellers, we let them know up from we expect to make a profit, and for us to make a profit we need to be able to stop the foreclosure. There is no charge for our services and the only way we make a profit is if we can stop the foreclosure. By being direct, the seller understands our incentive and motivation and this helps establish trust and rapport. When dealing with pre-foreclosures there are three main ways to profit:

1. **Purchase Property From Seller At A Discount.** Many times, a seller is willing to sell the property well below market value because they recognize it is better to cut their losses and move on instead of hanging on and going down with the ship. If the seller has enough equity, we can structure a purchase where they receive cash at closing, the balance of their equity in payments, or balloon payment due at a later date.

This can be a good option for sellers with enough equity. Unfortunately, in today's society the majority of seller owe close to the value of the property and when an investor takes into account acquisition costs, sales cost, holding costs, and repairs there is not enough equity in the property for an investor to make a profit.

2. **Take Over The Loan And Make Up Back Payments.** When a seller is in foreclosure it is possible to buy the house from the seller, take over the loan, and make up the back payments. The advantages for the seller are the foreclosure is stopped and the property is sold to an investor that will make the payments. A drawback for the seller is the loan remains in their name until paid off by the investor or a third party at a later date.

    The process of buying a home and taking over a loan in another person's name is commonly referred to as buying a property "subject to." In such a transaction, the title of the property transfer to the new owner, but the loan remains in the seller's name. Lending institutions frown on buying properties "subject to" and include a due on sale clause stating the lender can call the loan due upon a transfer of title. In practice, lenders rarely enforce a due on sale clause and are more interested in receiving timely payments then enforcing calling the loan due. Selling "subject to" is not without risks to the seller since the loan remains in their name and if payments are not made their credit can be affected at a later date. The benefits for the investor are acquiring a property with little money out-of-pocket, no loan costs or appraisal fees, and their credit is not affected or put at risk by the loan they are taking :subject to." This is a powerful investing strategy unknown to most investors and one that should be sued by ethical individuals. Like many powerful tools, it has the ability to be sued for good or bad depending on the individual. When purchasing "subject to" there are documents that must be signed for the protection and understanding of all involved.

3. **Discount The Loan(s) From The Lenders.** Commonly referred to as a "Short Sale" this is nothing more than negotiating with the lenders to accept an amount less than they are currently owed. A fair question is why would lenders discount their loans? There are a couple of reasons. 1) Lenders do not want to own properties. If a borrower does not pay the loan, a lender's recourse is to foreclose on the property and if they property is not bought at public auction they become the new owner of the property. Lenders are in the business of loaning money and when a loan is not being paid, it is considered a non-performing asset and affects their lending ratios. Also, as owner of the property, the bank is responsible for property taxes, insurance, association fees, Realtor commissions, and closing costs. 2) Cash now is better than cash later. Many times a bank would prefer the certainty of accepting a discount instead of the unknown holding costs, liability, and unknown sales price at a future date. The bank understands that a discounted offer today could net them more than a higher offer date when considering the closing costs, Realtor fees, and lost opportunities of lending money based on their ratios.

Whether buying a property "subject to" or attempting a short sale, you want to complete many of the same documents. Since short sales can be a lot of work before we begin, we hold title to the property "subject to" before negotiating with the lender. Experience has taught us the painful lesson of working months on a project and having everything worked out with the lenders, only to have a previously cooperative seller change their mind and refuse to complete the transaction. Trust our experience on their one.

The following documents are necessary and accompanied with a brief explanation:

1. **Standard Purchase and Sales Agreement & Escrow Instructions:** This document sets forth the terms of the sale.
2. **Authorization to Release Information:** This document allows us to contact the bank, discuss the property and the loan, and work out payment/payoff arrangements.
3. **Letter Of Agreement and Addendum:** This document clarifies that we will do our best to stop the foreclosure, but are unable to make any guarantees. We will not make promises we are unable keep.
4. **Warranty Deed To Trustee:** This document conveys ownership of the property. Must be signed before a notary.
5. **Agreement and Declaration of Trust:** This document creates the land trust. A land trust is nothing more than an entity we use to title the property and keep our name off public records.
6. **Letter That Trustee is Making Payments:** This letter is used when taking property "subject to" and notifies the lender that payment will becoming from a trustee.
7. **Escrow Letter:** This letter instructs the lender to apply to funds in any escrows account to the loan balance when the loan is paid in full. There is not guarantee the lender will comply with the instructions and they may send the escrow proceeds to the original borrower.
8. **Special Power of Attorney:** Applies only to the property and is used to handle any situations that may arise. Must be signed before a notary.

9. **Residential Real Estate Disclosure:** Discloses any defects in the property and prevents parties from saying, "I did not know about that defect." Complies with state law.

10. **Hardship Letter:** When dealing with foreclosures, the lender normally requires a letter from the borrower explaining their hardship and why they are unable to make the payments.

11. **Financial Statement:** Before discounting a loan and taking a known loss, the lenders will want to review the original borrower's financial statement and make sure the borrower does not have the ability to repay the debt now or in the foreseeable future.

When preparing a short sale, lenders require a short sale package before they will consider accepting a discount. We recommend you provide the following documents:

1. **Cover Letter:** A letter requesting a short sale and why the lender should consider your offer.
2. **Authorization to Release Information**
3. **Standard Real Estate Purchase and Sale Agreement**
4. **Hardship Letter from Borrower**
5. **Financial Statement From Borrower**
6. **Proposed Closing Statement (HUD1):** All lenders want to see a HUD1 so they know their bottom line and to ensure the seller is not receiving any compensation.
7. **Opinion Of Value:** We recommend you provide the lowest comparable sales in the area.
8. **Estimate of Repairs:** Most properties need repairs, and if you expect the lender to discount you need to detail the necessary repairs.
9. **Notice of Trustee's Sale:** The actual foreclosure notice should be included and subtly lets the lender know you understand the foreclosure process.

10. **Color Photos:** Supply the lender with photos of all problems on the property. This helps the lender justify accepting a lower price for the property.

Short sales provide a great opportunity for creating equity and can be done with out risking your cash and without using your credit. By negotiating discounts with the lender, you can create a situation where the property can be purchased well below market value and other investors will purchase this opportunity from you and close the transaction with cash! Everyone wins: the seller has the foreclosure stopped and may receive some of their equity, the lender receives a negotiated amount of cash a closing, the investor that purchases the property is able to buy at a below-market price, and you receive a well-deserved profit for your negotiating skills and ability to put the transaction together. Or, you can always buy the property yourself.

This chapter was contributed by Gerald Romine. Gerald is an active investor, educator, and speaker and can be contacted at www.azpig.com, Gerald@azpig.com, or by calling 480-461-6059.

Available Resources

Available Resources

The following books, videos, and audio cassettes have been reviewed by the Liberty Network staff and are suggested as reading and resource material for continuing education to help with your real estate and stock market investments. Because new ideas and techniques come along and laws change, we're always updating our catalogue.

To order a copy of our current catalogue,
please write or call us at:

Liberty Network, Inc.
1420 N.W. Gilman Blvd. #2131
Issaquah, Washington 98027
1-866-579-5900

Or, visit us on our web site at
www.wadecook.org

Also, we would love to hear your comments on our products and services, as well as your testimonials on how these products have benefited you. We look forward to hearing from you!

Stock Market

Income Formulas-A Free CD
By Wade B. Cook

Learn the 11 cash flow formulas taught in the Wall Street Workshop. Learn to double your money every 21/2 to 4 months.

Wall Street Money Machine
By Wade B. Cook

Appearing on the New York Times Business Best Seller list for over one year, Wall Street Money Machine contains the best strategies for wealth enhancement and cash flow creation you'll find anywhere. Throughout this book, Wade Cook describes many of his favorite strategies for generating cash flow through the stock market: Rolling Stock, Proxy Investing, Covered Calls, and many more. It's a great introduction for creating wealth using the Wade Cook formulas.

Stock Market Miracles
By Wade B. Cook

The anxiously-awaited partner to Wall Street Money Ma-chine, this book is proven to be just as invaluable. Stock Market Miracles improves on some of the strategies from Wall Street Money Machine, as well as introducing new and valuable twists on our old favorites. This is a must read for anyone interested in making serious money in the stock market.

Zero To Zillions
By Wade B. Cook

This is a powerful audio workshop on Wall Street-under-standing the stock market game, playing it successfully, and retiring rich. Learn eleven powerful investment strategies to avoid pitfalls and losses, catch "day-trippers," "bottom fish," write covered calls, double your money in one week on options on stock split companies, and so much more. Wade "Meter Drop" Cook will teach you how he makes 300% per year, so that you can do likewise.

The Wall Street Workshop Video Series
By Wade B. Cook

If you can't make it to the Wall Street Workshop soon, get a head start with these videos. Ten albums containing eleven hours of intense instruction on rolling stock, options on stock split companies, writing covered calls, and eight other tested and proven strategies designed to help you earn 18% per month on your investments. By learning, reviewing, and implementing the strategies taught here, you will gain the knowledge and the confidence to take control of your investments, and double their value every 2 to 4 months.

Dynamic Dollars DVD
By Wade B. Cook

Wade Cook's 90 minute introduction to the basics of his Wall Street formulas and strategies. In this presentation designed

Wealth Information Network (WIN)

This subscription computer bulletin board service provides you with the latest financial formulas and updated entity structuring strategies. New, timely information is entered Monday through Friday, sometimes four or five times a day. Wade Cook and his Team Wall Street staffwrite for WIN, giving you updates on their own current stock plays, companies who announced earnings, companies who announced stock splits, and the latest trends in the market.

WIN is also divided into categories according to specific strategies and contains archives of all our trades so you can view our history.

Entity Integration

Power Of Nevada Corporations CD
By Wade B. Cook

Nevada Corporations have secrecy, privacy, minimal taxes, no reciprocity with the IRS, and protection for shareholders, officers, and directors. This is a powerful seminar.

The Incorporation Handbook
By Wade B. Cook

Incorporation made easy! This handbook tells you who, why, and, most importantly, how to incorporate. Included are samples of the forms you will use when you incorporate, as well as a step-by-step guide from the experts.

The Financial Fortress Home Study Course
By Wade B. Cook

This eight-part series is the last word in entity structuring. It goes far beyond mere financial planning or estate planning, and helps you structure your business and your affairs so that you can avoid the majority of taxes, retire rich, escape lawsuits, bequeath your assets to your heirs without government interference, and, in short-bomb proof your entire estate. There are six audio cassette seminars on tape, an entity structuring video, and a full kit of documents.

Real Estate

Income Streams-A free CD
By Wade B. Cook
Learn to buy and sell real estate the Wade Cook way. This informative cassette will instruct you in building and operating your own real estate money machine.

Owner Financing
By Wade B. Cook

This is a short but invaluable pamphlet you can give to sellers who hesitate to sell you their property using the owner financing method. Let this pamphlet convince both you and them. The special report, "Why Sellers Should Take Monthly Payments," is included for free!

Real Estate Money Machine
By Wade B. Cook

Wade's first bestselling book reveals the secrets of Wade Cook's own system—the system he earned his first million from. This book teaches you how to make money regardless of the state of the economy. Wade's innovative concepts for investing in real estate not only avoid high interest rates, but avoid banks altogether.

Real Estate For Real People
By Wade B. Cook

A priceless, comprehensive overview of real estate investing, this book teaches you how to buy the right property for the right price, at the right time. Wade Cook explains all of the strategies you'll need, and gives you twenty reasons why you should start investing in real estate today. Learn how to retire rich with real estate, and have fun doing it.

101 Ways To Buy Real Estate Without Cash
By Wade B. Cook

Wade Cook has personally achieved success after success in real estate. 101 Ways to Buy Real Estate Without Cash fills the gap left by other authors who have given all the ingredients but not the whole recipe for real estate investing. This is the book for the investor who wants innovative and practical methods for buying real estate with little or no money down.

Legal Forms
By Wade B. Cook

This collection of pertinent forms contains numerous legal forms used in real estate transactions. These forms were selected by experienced investors, but are not intended to replace the advice of an attorney. However, they will provide essential forms for you to follow in your personal investing.

Record Keeping System
By Wade B. Cook

A complete record keeping system for organizing all of the information on each of your properties. This system keeps track of everything from insurance policies to equity growth. You will know at a glance exactly where you stand with your investment properties and you will sleep better at night.

Brilliant Deductions
By Wade B. Cook

Do you want to make the most of the money you earn? Do you want to have solid tax havens and ways to reduce the taxes you pay? This manual is for you! Learn how to get rich in spite of the new tax laws. See new tax credits, year-end maneuvers, and methods for transferring and controlling your entities. Learn to structure yourself and your family for tax savings and liability protection.

Appendix

Why is this stock markket information in a real estate book? Wade has an incredible desire to teach and help people. You who know him, know he can teach real estate, asset protection, business, marketing, nine variations of stock market trading-and his students have and will continue to benefit. However, over the past fifteen years he has worked on and perfected an income strategy that everyone could and should use. It is "writing covered calls" -with all of its repetitive cash flow variations. Everyone needs extra income. Most don't have the time or inclination to develop the skills. Here are two questions: (1) Can you spare one to three hours a month, and (2) Do you need extra cash flow?

If you answered yes to both of these questions, you might want to take a look at the following information. This program could help you generate extra cash to help you in your real estate business.

JOB FREE INCOME
(Title of a CD Seminar by Wade Cook)

Question: If $5,000 could produce $1,000 to $2,000 cash every month-would you be interested in learning how?

Question: Do you know how to treat the stock market like a business?

Question: Could the stock market be the answer to your cash flow needs? Do you know how to get assets to produce your income so you can quit your job?

LIBERTY NETWORK INC.

Is happy and pleased to introduce you to...

WADE COOK
Four Times, New York Times Business
Bestselling Author of Wall Street Money
Machine, Business Buy the Bible, Stock
Market Miracles, and Wade Cook's Stock
Picking Handbook.

Join Wade Cook, in three remarkable experiential learning formats. These services are here to help you grow your wealth-DESIGNED TO GET YOU A SECOND PAYCHECK WITHOUT GETTING A SECOND JOB.

TNT: TUESDAY NIGHT TRAINING
TDT: THOUSAND DOLLAR THURSDAY
TST: TRADING SKILLS for TODAY

T N T
TUESDAY NIGHT TRAINING

- Investing vs. Trading
- Monthly Income
- Real Deals
- Writing Covered Calls
- Avoiding Problems

Liberty Network Inc. lets you, from the comfort of your home, join with Wade Cook (our lead instructor) and other top educators, investors and traders, in a lively evening presentation. 6PM Pacific, 9PM Eastern.

These events are simply wonderful:

- Techniques
- Actual Trades-5 to 10 each week
- Street-wise tips, formulas & methods

These remarkable evening presentations are designed to help you increase your wealth and enhance your cash flow.

Regular Price: $25 per Event-Now just $44 For a WHOLE Month.

T S T
TUTORING SKILLS for TODAY

Look over the shoulder of Wade Cook and our Team Wallstreet as they do their trades. We also help you paper trade to really learn each technique and develop confidence.

- Explore, learn and earn
- See money made as it happens
- Log on 24/7-at your convenience
- Connect-the-Dots-See Wade and the team make the deals
- Win-Lose-Draw-our trades, with "WHY" and "HOW" commentary are given to help you when you need the help.

Here's how it works: As a Subscriber, you will receive a PIN and PASSWORD. Just log on and see the deals done. Frequent (5 to 10 entries) are made every day. We're here to help you get your ASSETS PRODUCING CASH FLOW! Yes, every month.

This service is $200 per month, But now, FREE with your $44 TNT subscription.

T D T
THOUSAND DOLLAR THURSDAY

$$ A GRAND NEW DEAL EVERY DAY $$
$1,000 $1,000 $1,000 $1,000

You've heard the adage - "Teach a Man to Fish…" As the company that under-promises and over-delivers, we go one step further. WE GET THE FISH JUMPING IN YOUR BOAT.

Recent TDT (Trades)

STSI	$3,200	made	$850
CTIC	$4,990	made	$2,200
ENCY	$4,995	made	$1,800
NGEN	$2,400	made	$550
RMBS	$6,900	made	$3,420

We'll E-MAIL YOU SO YOU CAN STAY IN THE LOOP.
We will send you a trading technique-exploring methods and actual trades-every Thursday. TDT is usually one page, sometimes more. TDT gives you the deals with "in-the-trenches" explanations.

We usually use $5,000 to make $1,000 or more. If you have $1,000 or $25,000 to use - just adjust your trades. Then check out TST for more trades and explanations.

PRICE: $495 a year (and worth every penny), But now FREE with TNT.
HOW DO YOU LEARN BEST?

Do you like to read? Do you like to watch DVD's and videos? Do you like to do the deals yourself?

We're Here for You!!

No Motivational lectures, no namby-pamby information. We share "industrial strength" knowledge to help you make more money!

Just Think-Everything you have learned how to do, and do well, you were hand trained by someone else. Now you can use Wade Cook as your "cash flow mentor".

HOW DO YOU LEARN BEST?

Do you like to read? Do you like to watch DVD's and videos? Do you like to do the deals yourself?

We're Here for You!!

No Motivational lectures, no namby-pamby information. We share "industrial strength" knowledge to help you make more money!

Just Think-Everything you have learned how to do, and do well, you were hand trained by someone else. Now you can use Wade Cook as your "cash flow mentor".

JOIN WITH US: TNT, TST, TDT

For more information please contact:
1-866-579-5900

Thoughts from Wade Cook

"The money is in the meter drop.
You get in, you get out. You make money."

"Our purpose in life should be
to build a life of purpose."

"If you'll do for two years what most people won't do,
you'll be able to do for the rest of your life
what most people can't do."

"The greatest good we can do for others is not to share our
riches, but to help them uncover and find theirs."

"Success comes from you, not to you."

"Virtually every major achievement, indeed, every major change has its genesis in the thoughts and actions of a single man or woman. Then the team helps bring it to fruition. Are you the one to make major changes in your life? Are you the one to lead, to lift and inspire your friends? Are you the one God needs to bring about much good? Are you a force for good?"

"Our thoughts become our actions; our actions become our habits; our habits control our destiny."

"Reward what you want to see more of. Celebrate small achievements. Make people feel important, though the accomplishments be small. Find worthwhile excuses to party."

"I have build my life in loving and educating people and pray only that someone can stand on my shoulders and reach a higher level."

"What in life inspires daily noble actions? What is it that delights the heart, stirs the soul, swells the breast and seeks companionship for sharing? Simply this, Discovery."